Leading
the Association

Striking the Right Balance Between Staff and Volunteers

James J. Dunlop

Published by The Foundation of the
American Society of Association Executives
and made possible by a grant
from Loews Anatole Hotel

Cover Design: Design Consultants, Inc.,
        Falls Church, Virginia
Design: Bremmer & Goris Communications,
        Alexandria, Virginia

Editor: Heidi H. Bowers, ASAE, Washington, D.C.

Composition: Herz Type, Springfield, Virginia

Proofreading: Editorial Experts, Inc., Alexandria, Virginia

Printing: St. Mary's Press, Hollywood, Maryland

Library of Congress Cataloging-in-Publication Data

Dunlop, James J.
  Leading the association.

  1. Trade and professional associations—United States—
Management. 2. Associations, institutions, etc.—United States
—Management. 3. Voluntarism —United States—Management.
I. American Society of Association Executives. Foundation.
II. Title.
HD2425.D86   1989   060′.68   89–16895
ISBN 0–88034–038–X

American Society of Association Executives
1575 Eye Street, N.W.
Washington, D.C. 20005–1168

Printed in the United States of America

Contents

Foreword

Each association must identify and analyze trends unique to its particular constituency and market. Most, however, cannot afford the time, effort, and money to produce information on general association and national trends. It is to this area that The Foundation of the American Society of Association Executives is committed and from which *Leading the Association: Striking the Right Balance Between Staff and Volunteers* derives.

In the early 1960s, several visionary association executives met to discuss the opportunities and challenges of association management. They articulated the need to plan, coordinate, and conduct a variety of projects critical to the long-term growth of the profession. The Foundation of the American Society of Association Executives, established in 1963, has adopted this important mission.

Each year The Foundation identifies areas for research and produces studies to give the association community information about the trends and issues that will affect its future and to provide a solid intellectual basis for the profession. Underwritten by a generous grant from Loews Anatole Hotel, Dallas, *Leading the Association: Striking the Right Balance Between Staff and Volunteers* will help individual associations realize brighter futures, aid executives and volunteers in shaping those futures, and increase the high level of professional competence that has become a hallmark of association management.

This work delineates for the first time the unique characteristics of staff-driven and volunteer-driven associations, identifies specific strategies for shifting from one leadership mode into another, and explores the developmental patterns of associations that create these emphases. We are confident that *Leading the Association* will become a landmark piece of literature by augmenting the general understanding of associations.

Charles D. Rumbarger, CAE   Lee VanBremen, Ph.D., CAE
Task Force on Staff and Volunteer Influence
The Foundation of the American Society of Association Executives
Washington, D.C.   May 1989

Preface

This book is about the influence of volunteers and staff in associations. Its purpose is to shed light on the relationships between volunteer and staff leaders and how and why these roles differ from one association to another. The book covers trade associations;* professional societies, including engineering and scientific societies; and philanthropic associations,** including health-related and social service organizations. It examines associations of national, state, and local geographic scopes.[1]

Recognizing that the source of initiative or influence is an issue of continuing concern in associations, the Foundation of the American Society of Association Executives commissioned this study in 1987. Its hope was that a careful examination of the characteristics of staff- and volunteer-driven associations, the unique ways these associations function, the benefits and drawbacks of each leadership mode, and specific actions that leaders can take to alter an unsatisfactory situation would be useful to many staff executives and volunteer leaders.

The study thus explores the similarities and differences between staff-driven and volunteer-driven associations and describes a

---

*For the purposes of statistical analysis, trade associations were broken into two categories: 1) that group of associations traditionally regarded as trade associations, comprising business firms or organizations as members, and 2) a group of business-based associations whose members comprise individuals engaged in a trade or a business pursuit. Each survey respondent selected a category best describing his or her association, whether trade with organizational members, trade with individual members, professional society, or philanthropic association. Examples of trade associations with individual members are the National Association of Realtors and the National Association for Hospital Development.

**Organizations that are patron- or client-oriented such as museums, hospitals, libraries, and symphony orchestras are not included in this book, although some of the findings may be applicable to them.

third leadership mode of influence balanced between staff and volunteers. *Driven* refers to the predominant influence of one group over another. An association is said to be volunteer-driven when policy or new program initiatives emanate predominantly from volunteers and when volunteers make the major decisions about the direction and operation of ongoing programs and activities. An association is considered to be staff-driven when initiatives originate predominantly from the staff and when the staff make the major decisions. In associations with a balanced influence, staff and volunteers initiate in roughly equal proportions, although often in different realms. Also included are suggestions for determining the source of influence and for shifting it, if needed, to permit the association to function more effectively.

Research formed the basis for the book. The research involved personal interviews with the chief staff executives (CSEs) and volunteer leaders of 22 associations and covered a wide range of topics related to the history and functioning of each association, the degree to which the association is staff- or volunteer-driven, and the factors that made it so.

Two surveys augmented the interviews. The first, mailed to 1,000 trade associations and professional societies, generated a 23 percent response rate (234 associations). The second, sent to 889 philanthropic associations, had a response rate of 20 percent (184 associations). Summary results of the surveys are presented throughout the book.

The book primarily addresses association executives, those individuals who live day by day, year in, year out with their associations and who help to maintain the continuity and integrity of their organizations as volunteer leaders come and go. Nevertheless, volunteer leaders may also be interested, particularly those who want to alter the balance to include more staff direction or to assert more volunteer influence in an organization that is too staff dependent. Senior staff as well may find the survey results and perspectives offered useful as aids in understanding their roles and in facilitating their work.

Of particular interest to CSEs are the detailed discussions of the CSEs' relationships in associations and their role in changing leadership mode. Future trends are presented for the benefit of all those involved in managing associations to help them develop strategies for the decades to come.

Acknowledgments

A cast of talented people made this work possible through their expertise, advice, and support. Loews Anatole Hotel, Dallas, Texas, underwrote the research and writing costs through a grant to The ASAE Foundation.

Special acknowledgment is due to the task force of The ASAE Foundation that had oversight responsibilities for this project. The committee members comprised Charles Rumbarger, CAE, president, Association Management Group, Washington, D.C., and Lee VanBremen, Ph.D., CAE, executive vice president, American Academy of Facial Plastic and Reconstructive Surgery, Washington, D.C. These men underpinned this project with their time and energies, providing invaluable support and constructive criticism.

Several among the ASAE staff also deserve mention: R. William Taylor, CAE, president, for his commitment to this study and thorough review of the manuscript; Elissa M. Myers, CAE, director of the publishing division, for her thoughtful and helpful suggestions; Ann Kenworthy, manager of The ASAE Foundation, for her careful project coordination; Heidi H. Bowers, book editor, for fine-tuning the manuscript; Elizabeth Malloy, manager of book publishing, for overseeing production; and Eric Johnson, former manager of The ASAE Foundation, for his aid in the project's early stages.

Gratitude also is due to Homer J. Hagedorn, Ph.D., a former colleague with Arthur D. Little, Inc., for reviewing drafts and offering valuable suggestions to improve content and style.

Survey research was conducted by Dorr Research Corporation, Boston, Massachusetts; assistance in interviewing by Alexandra Clark, Marston Mills, Massachusetts, and Sarah Kingsbury, Boston; and editorial assistance by Miriam d'Amato, Professional Editorial Service, Winthrop, Massachusetts. Thanks to each for the valuable help.

A final acknowledgment goes to the author's wife, Judy, whose support, encouragement, forbearance, and insistence on planning ahead kept the task of writing from being all work.

Chapter 1

Introduction

Associations are unique, both in purpose and organization. They are not businesses, although they can be run in a businesslike fashion. They do not function like hospitals or universities, although they may raise millions of dollars for health research and service and offer extensive continuing education activities. They are not social welfare agencies, although they are almost always not for profit and may operate broadly in the public interest. They are not government agencies, although they may influence the process of government and frequently stand in for government in such areas as standards and certification.

The Purpose of Associations

Each American is a part of one or more special interest groups. Particular affiliations are based on a person's workplace, beliefs, profession, political affiliation, and individual attributes. Most adult Americans are formal members of one or more special interest groups for political, professional, business, personal, or ideological reasons. Associations permit special interests of all kinds to be identified and heard.

Empowering the Members

By comprising groups of individuals and organizations that have banded together voluntarily because of their common

1

interest, associations occupy a unique and necessary niche in our democracy. While they have many functions, their essential purpose is to empower their members. By themselves, the individuals and organizations that make up an association have relatively little power. In association, however, they are able to exert influence and obtain information in ways that are not possible for the individual acting alone.

Influence with the larger society is gained through lobbying, promulgating ideas, mobilizing public opinion, and, for many associations, creating product or professional standards that come to have the force of law. Having influence in the larger society, however, is based largely on the association's ability to influence its own members.[2] Effective associations do both. In order for an association to advocate a position on a public issue, for example, the members must first be in substantial accord on that position. In order to reach accord, particularly on controversial issues, some members must shift their views and modify their positions. If the association is able to accomplish such shifts and thereby achieve an agreed-upon stance internally, then it can effectively represent a position externally to the government at national, state, and local levels; to other organizations and institutions; or to the public. Thus, the process of influence works both ways, internally as well as externally. *How well that process works depends, to a great extent, on the relationships among the volunteer leaders and the staff.*

Associations influence their members in many ways, among them, through programs of education and training, meetings, committee activities, information exchange, codes of conduct, awards, publications, correspondence, and grass-roots support for positions.

When the members comply with requests by their association to write their representatives, to march, or to boycott, the result is political power. Members are voters, and politicians pay attention to voters, particularly blocs of voters. When the National Association of Realtors (NAR) advocates retaining the deductibility of home mortgage interest for income tax purposes and its members contact their legislators in support of the association's position, NAR can be an infinitely more effective advocate than a broker-member acting alone, regardless of the size of that person's firm.

Although individual corporate members of an association may have financial resources that far exceed the resources of the association itself, they do not have the currency that most impresses legislators—votes. An individual member may know a particular legislator more intimately than the professional lobbyists of an association, but that member usually cannot know all the legislators important to a particular piece of legislation or the cast of characters that shifts with different pieces of legislation. The association can. Moreover, the association can claim to speak for the industry, profession, or interest group as a whole. The individual cannot.

It would be naive in the extreme to assume that corporate or individual members always act through their associations or that they do not themselves have access to the political process. In our country, however, that sort of influence is moderated by the existence of associations. In some very important ways, the existence of associations helps keep alive the democratic process on which our nation is built. Consider the words of French statesman and author Alexis de Tocqueville.

> Among the laws that rule human societies there is one which seems to be more precise and clear than all others. If men are to remain civilized, or to become so, the art of associating together must grow and improve in the same ratio in which the equality of conditions is increased.[3]

Associations, when they work well, represent a unified voice, not many voices singing various tunes. Members of an industry acting independently can be a cacophony to be dismissed and its members to be played off against one another. A unified voice gets heard. When life insurance companies agree on a position, their association is extremely effective in getting their point across to legislators at the federal and state levels. When they cannot agree and have to go it alone on a company-by-company basis, they often speak at cross-purposes and, thus, less effectively.

Associations also influence public opinion and the actions of other groups. The American Bar Association can change public opinions about nominees to the U.S. Supreme Court, thereby indirectly influencing how senators will vote in confirmation hearings. The Risk and Insurance Management Society (RIMS), the association of risk managers in corporations and other organizations, has much to say about the types of property and casualty insurance made available to businesses, and property and casualty insurance companies pay attention to RIMS.

Philanthropic organizations, such as the American Cancer Society and the National Multiple Sclerosis Society, also exert influence and represent a concentration of power. Health-oriented philanthropic associations use their influence, in part, to persuade individuals to contribute money to fight, conquer, and eradicate diseases or medical conditions or to alter their living habits to become healthier. Many of these organizations also influence the government by advocating larger budgets for such federal organizations as the National Institutes of Health or the Centers for Disease Control and by promoting legislation in line with their causes. Other philanthropic associations, such as the YMCA and the American Red Cross, attempt to influence public opinion to favor their causes, such as physical fitness, water safety, and blood donations.

It is probably accurate to say that all associations are in the business of influence to a considerable degree. While they also provide services to their members and the public, publish journals, and carry on other activities, their primary function is to exert influence, both externally on their environment and internally on their members.

How is this influence exercised? Associations, as a rule, have neither great financial resources nor police powers and, therefore, cannot directly reward or punish very effectively. Consequently, they must exercise influence in the only other available way: through articulating and promulgating ideas.[4] Ideas are their only real, dependable instrument for wielding influence. No other institution in our society has the franchise that associations have to formulate and promulgate ideas concerning an industry, profession, or cause. It is through ideas that associations can lead.

Associations can and do espouse ideas that will further their cause, and they expect that these ideas will enter into general currency.[5] Some associations have done this with remarkable success. One has only to look at Common Cause, Mothers Against Drunk Driving, or the American Lung Association to see how powerfully ideas can be made to work for an association and its members.

The Role of Education

Education, an activity common to many associations, deserves special mention. Courses, seminars, presentations, and associated materials are a principal means for an association to influence its members in conducting their business or profession. Education can also be and indeed is a significant source of income for associations, especially professional associations. For some, such as the American Management Association, education is the primary activity.

Association education programs define standard practices in many industries and indicate what skills and knowledge are necessary to keep practicing in many professions. Courses, seminars, and programs at conventions all help to keep professionals up to date on developments in their fields and business executives current on management techniques and technical developments in their industries. Associations help to educate production-level workers in industries such as pharmaceuticals and metalworking, middle-level managers in areas such as personnel and financial management, top executives in techniques of management, and professionals in the engineering and scientific disciplines by providing information on new discoveries and techniques. Many philanthropic associations carry on extensive education programs for their professional and lay members in areas ranging from health to political action.

The Emergence of Association Management

Despite the ubiquity of associations and the fact that most people belong to at least one, relatively little exists in the management literature about how they function, how they are organized, how they are governed, or how to shift influence between staff and volunteers. Association management has only in the past decade been recognized as a legitimate field of study. Graduate schools have just recently begun to offer courses in the management of not-for-profit organizations, but many of these focus on the management of hospitals and universities, not on associations. Courses specifically dealing with association management are offered cooperatively in Washington, D.C. by the University of Maryland and the American Society of Association Executives (ASAE) and throughout the country by ASAE's allied and affinity societies. George Washington and De Paul Universities offer master's degrees in association management. Despite these programs, the actual body of knowledge about the leadership, management, and organization of associations is quite small. ASAE, both directly and through its foundation, and the Chamber of Commerce of the United States are gradually rectifying this situation by adding to the literature of association management and developing education programs for association executives. Progress is steady but slow.

In part, the paucity of information and analysis stems from the fact that associations have historically operated with small staffs and budgets. Until recently, very few associations had annual revenues of more than $5 million or staffs of 100 or more, according to one standard reference. In 1980, for example, only 110 national trade and professional associations (exclusive of unions) reported annual budgets of more than $5 million out of a total population of 5,300 associations listed in one directory of national trade and professional associations. Today, less than a decade later, more than 300 national associations report annual budgets of at least $5 million, as well as many state and local associations.[6]

Furthermore, associations are not as easily understood as businesses. While businesses exist primarily to create customers[7] and to earn money for their owners, the purposes of associations range widely from protecting the industry against burdensome government regulation to promoting research to conquer a chronic disease.

Moreover, the original purposes for which an association formed do not necessarily endure. A change in a law, new technology, the discovery of disease preventives and cures, affirmative action legislation, the development of a subspecialty, and a host of other changes can cause an association to radically alter its mission. The March of Dimes, organized in the 1930s to help victims of poliomyelitis, is perhaps the most famous example. When a vaccine to prevent polio was discovered in the 1950s, the purpose of the organization was no longer viable. Instead of going out of business, the March of Dimes turned its attention to birth defects and has been vigorous ever since.

Association management as a field of study and in its use of modern management techniques today stands at approximately the same stage of development as hospitals did 15 to 20 years ago; and hospital management then lagged the field of business management by about a generation. However, now, with increased recognition that associations constitute a major force in our economy (national trade and professional associations alone spend approximately $60.7 billion annually and employ more than 580,000 people, according to some estimates),[8] together with their increased visibility and a growing professionalism of their executives, the field is beginning to mature. Associations will never approach the collective economic power of corporations or government, but their influence requires that they be understood as significant economic, social, and political entities in their own right.

The Evolution of Associations

An association, as a rule, begins with a small group of people who have an affinity—members of an engineering discipline or an architectural specialty, business owners or managers, or individuals concerned about a problem. If these individuals are able to identify a sufficient number of others of like mind or circumstance, they may be able to start an association.

One founder coordinates initial communication among the other founding members on a volunteer basis. Printing, postage, the cost of meetings, and other expenses are reimbursed by the members, sometimes in the form of dues and sometimes as an assessment or a contribution. Because there is no full- or part-time staff, the association is volunteer-driven. Volunteers give their time to keeping the organization going and growing. Communication is the key to sustaining the group. An issue such as a legislative threat is invaluable to growth and to identifying other prospective members.

Eventually, if the organization grows to a size that makes communications among the members too burdensome and costly for volunteers to handle alone, hiring takes place to manage the correspondence and, perhaps, to coordinate the meetings. In some cases, these jobs are given to a multiple-management firm that handles several organizations, each on a part-time basis, and can realize economies of scale in, say, producing newsletters or handling accounts. In other cases, a part-time person is hired. If the association grows, the position eventually develops into full-time work.

The addition of paid staff changes the balance of influence in the association. However, even if paid staff handle a greater share of the administrative and operational work, the association may continue to be volunteer-driven, because the volunteers make the key decisions to allocate resources and take programmatic initiatives. Even in fairly large associations, the volunteers may retain responsibility for a significant portion of the association's operations, particularly those concerned with publications, meetings, and education. Volunteers also usually maintain control of the association's finances.

As the organization grows in membership, the range and variety of its activities will also increase to answer members' needs. Added functions such as education, publications, meetings management, advocacy, regional services, and so forth all require additional staff. Because they call for expertise and specialization, these additional functions will usually be staff operated, although they may be volunteer directed. As the functions become more technical (insurance is one example), staff will increasingly drive them, with or without volunteer oversight.

The growth of membership gives rise to complexity, which is reflected in the volunteer structure as well as in the staff organization. Volunteer committees form to handle the work of the volunteer members and often to oversee certain staff functions. These committees usually require staff support to handle correspondence, minutes, and logistics. How the working relationships develop between committees and the staff serving the committees helps to determine whether the association will be predominantly staff- or volunteer-driven, or a blend of both leadership modes.

The rate of growth of a trade or professional association in its early stages will be more rapid than the growth of its industry or profession as the association achieves initial penetration of its member market. Eventually, when a professional society includes about 50 percent of the eligible members in its profession or a trade association about 80 percent of the industry sales volume,* its growth will level out and parallel the growth of the profession or industry, just as corporate growth corresponds to the growth of markets in which the companies compete.

For philanthropic associations, the rate of growth is tied to public awareness of the cause for which the association was formed. While initial formation may involve only a handful of people, with sufficient publicity (planned or unplanned) growth in the early stages can be quite rapid. People with relevant concerns or problems are contacted through various other affiliations and solicited for membership and contributions. Growth following the early stages depends on the number of people who share the problem or concern and the degree of urgency for a solution. A mature philanthropic association may have several hundred thousand members and direct supporters and receive financial support from literally millions of people, as is the case with organizations such as the American Heart Association and the American Red Cross.

Structure: Setting the Stage for Influence

Most associations have a management and governance structure consisting of a board of directors or trustees (comprising

---

*These rules of thumb stem from the author's experience as a consultant to trade and professional associations and discussions with a wide range of association executives. Professional societies typically find it quite difficult to boost and retain membership beyond about 50 percent of the eligible members in a profession. Similarly, mature trade associations often find that their members are responsible for 80 percent or more of total industry sales, although they count as members only 50 to 60 percent of the firms in the industry.

representatives of the association's constituency) and paid staff to handle day-to-day business that the members cannot or will not handle with consistency. The board hires a chief staff executive who, in turn, hires and supervises the other paid staff. In most associations, provisions in the constitution or bylaws call for periodic turnover of the governing board through elections. Some philanthropic associations have self-perpetuating boards, although an individual's length of service on the board may be limited.

In the average trade or professional association surveyed for this study, an essentially new governing board takes office every four to five years. In the philanthropic associations surveyed, the board turns over approximately every six years. Key members of the paid staff may be in place for many years, thereby representing continuity for the association. The relationship of a changing volunteer leadership to a permanent staff is central to understanding how associations function, whether they are staff-driven or volunteer-driven, and why that issue is so important to those who direct and manage associations.

Members and Stakeholders

Trade and professional associations have members—organizations and individuals—who collectively make up the association and are the direct beneficiaries of its activities. Volunteer leaders are chosen from among the members, usually through elections. The governing board represents the members' interests and ensures that available funds and the activities supported by those funds benefit the members and their industry or profession.

Philanthropic associations may also have members (although many do not), but the association does not necessarily act to benefit them economically or professionally. Instead, the association functions on behalf of individuals with an illness or of a cause and therefore presumably acts in a larger public interest. Volunteer leaders are chosen from among those who are particularly interested in the cause and are willing to support the organization financially or otherwise. The governing board is a surrogate for society and represents the interests of people with the illness or the concern.

The members of a trade or professional association have a direct stake in the organization. They *are* the organization, at least in their business or professional lives, and, therefore, the association is of some direct economic consequence. The association exists to handle legislative or regulatory matters, to provide information and education, or to enhance the reputation and public acceptance of the members' activities.

The members of a philanthropic association have a stake in their organization, too, but usually of a different and less directly economic kind. Their stake is the cause for which the organization was founded and for which they donate their money and time. The association exists to support that cause, to raise money from members and others to advance the cause, and to provide information about and services useful to the cause for members and the public.

The differences in membership, benefits, and stakes between trade and professional associations on the one hand and philanthropic associations on the other show up in their leadership modes and how they are governed.

Volunteer-Driven and Staff-Driven Associations

To understand whether an association is staff- or volunteer-driven, one must know who directs it. For purposes of statistical analysis, the chief staff executives (CSEs) surveyed rated their organizations, publications, and income-generating services on a scale of 0 to 9, with 0 representing a totally volunteer-driven association and 9 a totally staff-driven association. These overall self-assessments were then checked against other information about the association, such as budgetary and personnel authority of the CSE, titles and designations of the chief executive officer, percentage of time the chief elected officer spends on association business, and degree to which publications and income-generating services were rated as staff- or volunteer-driven. By and large, the CSE's subjective overall ratings were very consistent with the more detailed assessments indicative of either a staff- or volunteer-driven leadership mode.

This study does not address nominal control exercised in a legalistic sense by the board or CSE but, rather, speaks of the actual direction of the affairs of the association. This distinction is important because the bylaws of most associations call for the board to exercise overall direction. The standard concept is for the board to make policy and for staff to carry it out. The way things actually work and who really runs the organization may, in fact, be quite different.

In a volunteer-driven association, volunteer leaders on the board and committees make basic decisions about the direction of the association and the allocation of resources. Volunteer committees often direct and guide staff activities. Committee chairs function as mini-chief elected officers with respect to the staff assigned to the committee and help determine the budgets of the staff departments over which they have supervision. Committee chairs frequently have veto power over the assignment or removal of staff, and their committees set basic policy affecting particular parts of the operation.

In a staff-driven association, the volunteer leaders serve more in an advisory capacity. The CSE guides the policy formulation of the association and is frequently the public spokesperson. Staff members make many basic decisions about the direction of the association and the allocation of resources. The volunteer members of the board may approve the decisions, but they are often asked to react to staff initiatives and are often told after the fact about changes that affect line items in the budget. Volunteer committees have little say in the operation of staff departments or in the development of policies that guide those departments, and staff committee assignments are not heavily influenced by the committees they serve.

An association operated by staff can be volunteer-driven, that is, staff members do the day-to-day, hands-on work, but volunteers provide direction and guidance and make the basic resource allocation decisions affecting activities.

Some organizations are both directed and operated by volunteers. Obviously, associations without a paid staff and those with small staffs rely on the work of volunteers to make things happen. In these cases, volunteers perform much of the actual work of the association, either singly or in committees. For example, the association may publish a newsletter that is compiled and edited by a volunteer and then distributed by staff to the members; or volunteers may run the education program by developing the curricula, recruiting the instructors, setting the educational policy, and doing the teaching. Volunteers may use staff to handle meeting logistics, produce the necessary promotional materials, and arrange for registration, but the volunteers operate the program.

Even in larger associations, volunteers may perform some of the operational duties, particularly those associated with education, publications, fund-raising, certification, and other activities that require volunteer expertise rather than association management experience. This is true in philanthropic associations where volunteers usually handle fund-raising through the direct solicitation of gifts.

Much of the distinction between the staff- and volunteer-driven leadership modes derives from the relative positions of the CSE and the chief elected officer. The CSE is hired by the association's board, and the chief elected officer is elected by the membership or the board, usually for one year. In a volunteer-driven association, the CSE often reports to the chief elected officer as his or her boss. The chief elected officer, representing the board and the membership, basically calls the shots for the year of office, and the CSE carries out that person's directions. Even in cases where there is a large staff, the chief elected officer may actually direct the association by initiating new programs, having a say in staff hirings and firings, calling staff meetings, and performing many other functions usually associated with the role of an established CSE.

Chapter 2

Key Issues Surrounding Leadership Mode

Questions about whether their associations are staff- or volunteer-driven frequently dominate discussions among chief staff executives (CSEs). How can CSEs generate more member participation? How can they give members the feeling that they are important to the functioning of the association. How can they make membership on the board more meaningful? CSEs also ask how they can moderate the annual swings that occur as each new chief elected officer seeks to leave a mark on the association. How can they eliminate or reduce the negative effects of having volunteer committees control the activities of parts of the staff, thereby fragmenting the association? These and similar issues all relate to the questions: To what extent is the association staff- or volunteer-driven, and can influence be adjusted, if necessary, better to enable the association to carry out its intended purposes?

Who Really Runs Things?

Understanding the distinctions between staff-driven and volunteer-driven associations is vital to every CSE and chief elected officer. The leadership mode colors every facet of the association's operation, including the functioning of the board, the position of the staff, and the relationships among officers, staff, and members. To administer a successful association —one that fulfills its stated purposes and thereby the needs of its members—the CSE should understand the association's dynamics. Learning how to make the association more or less staff-driven and how to permit the volunteers to take a greater or lesser role in directing affairs without sacrificing efficiency can be critical to an executive in guiding the development of the organization, to say nothing about keeping his or her job.

Many association executives take it on faith that associations should be volunteer-driven. After all, they think, "The association belongs to the members, not the staff." Others want more control by staff, feeling that a volunteer-driven association operates at cross-purposes or functions inefficiently. Still others advocate a blend, a partnership, where staff and volunteers function as peers, with the staff respected for their expertise and professional contributions.

In philanthropic associations, even though the turnover among volunteers tends to be slower than in trade or professional associations and the focus of activities is on particular groups of people or situations rather than on members, there are also differences of opinion about appropriate leadership roles for staff and volunteers. Executives often have questions about the role of volunteers and who directs the course of the organization. In some philanthropic associations, volunteers serve primarily as fund-raisers and the staff guide and manage them in that activity. In others, the volunteers take a more active role in directing the affairs of the organization, particularly if they have a personal stake in the organization or its area of concern.

Sources of Conflict

The issue of who should run the organization can be the source of great conflicts between staff and volunteers. By many accounts, these problems are the single greatest cause for the dismissal of CSEs, either because they attempt to exert too much influence in the organization's affairs or because they do not take sufficient responsibility for the association's functioning. For example, the CSE of one professional society, who was a member of the profession and served on the board of directors prior to his appointment, adopted the position that his responsibilities stopped with management of the staff. In his view, the CSE had no responsibility for the functioning and productivity of volunteer committees beyond assuring that they were staffed competently. He believed that the responsibility for the volunteer committees rested with the committee chairs and ultimately the elected president. A conflict arose because the volunteer leaders did not share his view. They expected the CSE to guide the activities of committees. The CSE's refusal to take more responsibility for the functioning of the entire association, including the volunteer structure, led eventually to his dismissal.

Even more common is the situation where the volunteers perceive that the staff, and the CSE in particular, influence too much. Volunteers may question how funds are spent or policy is made. Often, the board objects to the CSE informing them after the fact of a change or commitment rather than consulting them first. If the volunteer leaders are heavily shielded from staff activities, they may simply become suspicious. Their suspicions may trigger concerns in other areas, leading eventually to the question, "Who's running this place, anyhow?" At that point, life can become very difficult for the CSE, and if the situation is not rectified, he or she may soon be asked to resign.

In the case of one large trade association, the CSE, who was hired to take a stronger leadership role than his predecessor, developed a pattern of making significant decisions without involving the volunteer leaders except to inform them after the fact. The volunteers went along with his style for about two years, although a backlog of resentment was building, particularly among the younger board members who were not part of the old guard that had selected the CSE. Eventually, the CSE made one mistake too many and, because he lacked the board's support, was fired. After the fact, all comments about the situation related to the points that the CSE failed to involve the volunteer leaders in decisions, failed to build communication with them, and took too much authority into his own hands.

Problems seem to be particularly acute if an executive moves from a staff-driven trade association to a volunteer-driven professional society or vice versa. The leadership experience gained in one may, in some important respects, be a drawback in the other. The executive in a staff-driven trade association may place a high value on efficiency in getting the job done and a relatively low value on just how the decisions are made and who is involved. Those values, when translated to a volunteer-driven organization, may spell disaster.

In one case, a CSE who had formerly been with a trade group lasted only two years in his new position with a professional society before being asked to leave. He was replaced with a person from the association's profession who was seen to be more receptive to volunteer input and less insistent on having his own way. Volunteer leaders stated that the former executive had been unable to adapt to the culture of a professional society and did not seem to be able to work with volunteers.

The point of these examples is that the CSE's ability to handle the dynamics of the relationship between staff and volunteers, without being overwhelmed either by the desire to be in charge or the temptation to passively let the volunteers handle matters, is a prime requisite to keeping the job.

For those executives thinking about moving, it is imperative to understand the culture and leadership mode of the new association and to assess whether they have the skills and sensitivities to succeed. An executive used to taking a backseat to the volunteers is likely to find trouble ahead by going to work for an association where the CSE is required to be out front as a spokesperson. The same is true for executives who are used to taking a leadership role in their associations and who then move into a volunteer-driven association. Such a change may be a recipe for failure unless major adjustments are made.

Because associations of all kinds depend on a mix of volunteer and staff energies to function and because volunteer leaders change frequently, the relationship between staff and volunteers is always somewhat out of balance. Understanding the factors that influence that imbalance and the dynamic that results is essential to the health of the organization.

The situation can become very imbalanced when one side or the other is too passive or is excessively eager to control. Imbalance can also occur when either the volunteer or the staff leader is ideologically rigid or fixed on how things should be; for example, that staff should run the show; that volunteers must control the staff, because the leader views staff as an instrument; or that the CSE should report to the chief elected officer, who is the boss. These kinds of fixed positions conflict with the fact that the volunteer leaders change, and with each change, a new individual comes in with personal ideas about the relationships between staff and volunteers.

A Mandate for Change

When associations look for a new CSE, the search committee usually seeks a person with management and leadership skills. The skills sought, however, differ depending on whether the association has been staff- or volunteer-driven and on whether the volunteer leaders want to shift the leadership mode. Often, search committees do not make their requirements explicit; yet, it is crucial for the candidate to understand what is actually needed and actually sought. This is particularly true when the association is looking for someone to change the mode of leadership in order to increase the degree to which the staff take operational responsibility or to involve the volunteers more in decision making.

A surprising number of the CSEs surveyed said they were hired to make a change. In philanthropic associations, 25 percent of the executives who were able to explain why their organizations had become more staff-driven said they were hired to make the change. In trade and professional associations, the number is even higher—35 percent. Among associations that have become more volunteer-driven in the past decade, over 75 percent of the CSEs who gave a reason said that they have sought to increase volunteers' participation. In short, many CSEs who are hired to make a change do make a change. It follows, then, that in many situations where there is a change in the CSE, questions arise about how to orchestrate a desired shift in leadership mode.

The issue of leadership mode is of concern to volunteer leaders as well. Many volunteer leaders take their positions with little idea of how best to relate to the CSE or other senior staff members who have been with the association for many years. The models that most volunteer leaders draw on are their predecessors or members of their own business or profession. What predecessors did in the past may not be right for the association today. Indeed, a new volunteer leader may not even know that there are different models of staff-volunteer relationships.

Experience from other spheres may well be inapplicable, particularly for volunteer leaders trying to translate business experience into governing an association.

If the models of staff-volunteer relationships and associated leadership modes held by key volunteer leaders and the CSE are very different, then one or the other will inevitably be disappointed. The resulting frustration and anger can seriously disrupt the functioning of the association, and the effects can last for many years.

Chapter 3

Developmental Stages and Their Implications for Leadership Mode

Associations pass through fairly predictable stages in their development.[9] Chapter 1 presents a general pattern of the development and evolution of associations. This chapter explores in greater detail the five developmental stages—embryonic, growth, staff operation, maturity, and aging—and how each stage shapes the relationships between volunteers and staff.* The rate of change from one stage to the next is determined, depending on the type of association, by the growth of the association's industry or profession or by the intensity and duration of public concern about the cause and the ability of the association to raise donated funds.

Developmental Stages of Associations

Stage 1: Embryonic

Associations are formed by people who share a common interest in a profession, line of business, or concern and who are able to identify others with the same interests. In many cases, individuals are not aware of others who share their interest or concern until the association's founders articulate it and make it known.[10]

---

*This chapter draws upon the work of Arthur D. Little, Inc., Cambridge, Massachusetts, in describing the maturational stages of industries.

In 1981, for example, Mothers Against Drunk Driving (MADD) was formed by Candy Lightner, the mother of a 13-year-old girl who was killed in Fair Oaks, California, by a repeat-offender drunk driver. Lightner and a group of concerned citizens formed MADD to force effective and workable solutions to the drunk-driver problem and to assist the surviving victims of drinking and driving accidents. Before the organization was formed, many thousands of parents who were anguished by the loss of a child to a drunk-driving incident had no rallying point or sense of common identity. While concern about drunk driving was widespread, people felt it was largely a matter for the police and other law enforcement agencies. Then Candy Lightner decided to organize, and MADD was born. In just five years, MADD grew to be a nationwide organization with more than half a million supporters and members in 375 chapters and affiliates, including in Canada, New Zealand, and Great Britain.

Understanding the start-up or embryonic stage of an association is difficult without at the same time understanding the context of the industry, profession, or cause. Associations start because an industry, professional grouping, or cause is recognized, and people tied to the group or cause need to band together to communicate and to take action as a body that they cannot do alone. There is often a perceived legislative or regulatory threat or a problem evolving from an older, competing industry or profession, or other source.

The National Community Television Association, which ultimately became the National Cable Television Association, was formed, in part, to combat the threat of regulation by the Federal Communications Commission (FCC). Cable system operators, fearing what broadcasters and the FCC could do to their infant industry, banded together to form their own association to build some political muscle.

In most cases, one cannot easily identify the beginnings of an industry or profession because they are so often embedded in a related, older industry or profession. An industry in its embryonic stage may be distinct only to a few participants who discern a commonality or uniqueness that sets the nascent industry apart from its predecessor. For example, the advent of radio created the conditions for the electronics industry to differentiate from the electrical industry.

In a new or embryonic industry, while the growth rate may be accelerating, a meaningful rate cannot be calculated because the economic base is too small. As the number of competitors in an embryonic industry increases, making for the critical mass needed to form an association, these competitors can declare themselves to be an identifiable industry or a separate subset of a larger, older industry whose association is probably not paying sufficient attention to them. The market shares held by the principal competitors in the new industry are quite volatile and share is difficult to measure. Entry to the market is easy. There may be multiple competing technologies.

Similarly, a new profession may grow out of an older, more established one. Civil engineers, for example, broke from military engineers by turning their skills to civilian projects in peacetime, such as town walls and bridges. The fields of engineering and medicine have been particularly prolific as evidenced by the many societies representing various specialties. Alternatively, an allied or supportive function of a profession may form the basis for an independent association. The National Association of Emergency Medical Technicians, for example, was formed in 1975, just a few years after the EMT certificate was recognized in several states. Very often, an academic underpinning spurs individuals to identify readily with the emerging profession.

At the earliest stages, entry into the new profession is relatively easy, and formal education or certification requirements may be minimal. One's professional identity may be integrally tied to the organization where the person functions, rather than to the profession. This has been the case in many areas of management, such as personnel, public relations, benefits administration, and risk management. The new profession has little subspecialization and there are no recognized ancillaries. Indeed, the emerging profession may itself be ancillary to another older profession. The body of knowledge is small and fragmented, and much of what exists draws on other disciplines. The people involved feel the need to learn techniques from one another and have a strong desire to communicate the merits and usefulness of the emerging profession. There is usually considerable confusion and often some conflict about whether the new field merits the name of a discipline or profession, and members of the older profession may attempt to regulate or legislate it out of existence. This threat may be one of the principal reasons for forming a new association in the first place.

A new philanthropic association is often started by one individual or family who finds no organized effort to deal with a problem. In recent years, for example, associations have formed that deal with head injuries, Alzheimer's disease, myasthenia gravis, and a host of other disabling or life-threatening conditions. In the social welfare arena, dozens of national organizations with concerns ranging from the environment to illiteracy have formed in the space of just a few years. The founder may discover other individuals with the same concern through acquaintances, lists, advertisements, and publicity.

Whether an industry group, a professional society, or a cause-related alliance, the embryonic stages of most associations are similar. The founder communicates with others, money is tendered for memberships or as contributions, the group incorporates, and meetings are held to organize and establish ground rules. In the initial stages, the founders, all of whom are volunteers, handle organizing, communicating, conducting meetings, collecting money, and other basic functions. The association is volunteer-driven. The volunteers set the direction and do the work. They also usually devote major amounts of their time, energy, concern, and money to the new organization.

Particularly in the initial stages, there are frequent, major conflicts and uncertainties over the exact mission and role of the new organization and the strategies to pursue. There may be concerns about the erratic or irregular pace of development, the apparent overdependence on one or a few individuals, and the recurring feeling that it is just not worth the effort. Despite these concerns, the new organization moves ahead if the original organizers or their immediate successors are sufficiently committed and if enough new members or supporters can be found.

Stage 2: Growth

At some point, the founders or their successors realize that the basic tasks of communicating, organizing meetings, and administering a growing membership or donor base are becoming too much for them to handle. A paid secretary is needed, full- or part-time. In some cases, the volunteers hire a person to handle some of the work. In other cases, they retain a multiple association management firm. In the case of a philanthropic association, in particular, the founder may become the first paid staff member.

Hiring a paid staff person represents a significant change in leadership mode. A trade or professional association is still likely to be volunteer-driven in that the volunteer leaders take the initiatives, make basic decisions, and continue to handle much of the day-to-day work. Even so, the presence of a paid staff person begins the growth stage.

A good deal of uncertainty and experimentation characterize this stage. The volunteers are rarely clear about the kind of help they need, so the person or committee that does the hiring may not be explicit about the nature of the staff jobs to be done. Moreover, the people available to staff the struggling, underfunded, new association may not have the experience that enables them to ask crucial questions about the roles they are to assume and their accountability in those roles. Mutual dissatisfaction and high turnover often result.

Trade and professional associations in this stage are usually responding to growth in the industry or profession. For a trade association, the industry is expanding faster than the gross national product (GNP), a widely accepted standard. Product lines are undergoing rapid proliferation. The number of competitors is increasing, often resulting in a shakeout and consolidation down the road. Market entry is usually easy, and the presence of competitors is offset by vigorous growth.

In a professional society, the number of practitioners in the profession generally grows more rapidly than overall employment. Entry into the profession is still relatively easy, but pressure is beginning for certification and formal education requirements. Some subspecialization may be apparent, but basic identity remains with the principal profession. The members of the principal profession may exhibit hostility to the attempts of ancillary workers, such as technicians, to develop their own identity. The body of knowledge is growing, and there is likely to be a regular journal serving the field.

In a philanthropic association, there is recognition that the concern is significant. In the case of a philanthropic health association, a medical specialty may relate to the organization. Rheumatology, for example, is closely identified with the Arthritis Foundation. A social welfare association may experience significant growth in its membership and contributed income. People identify with the association in growing numbers and contribute money and time to further the cause.

As the industry, profession, or field of concern grows, the size and work of the association will increase also. To handle the increased work, more staff members are needed.

Increased specialization stems from staff growth. Administrative functions such as office management, bookkeeping, and answering telephones, and programmatic and member-oriented functions such as meetings, education, publications, and government affairs need to be staffed. At first, the staff are primarily concerned with facilitating the work of the volunteers who operate the functional aspects of the association—conducting and managing the education program or writing and publishing the newsletter and then the magazine. At some point, however, volunteer leaders realize that commitments are not being met, that the workload is too much for them to handle, and that performance is a concern. These conditions form the basis for staff operation, the next stage in the association's development.

Stage 3: Staff Operation

At this point in the life of a trade association or professional society, the volunteer leaders are convinced that staff need to do more of the work because of its sheer volume. They begin to turn over to staff some of the volunteer-run aspects of the organization so that programs formerly initiated by volunteers can continue even though their original proponents are gone. Many volunteers discover that they are sufficiently absorbed by their regular full-time jobs that they cannot give to the association the time required to continue programs and activities.

In a philanthropic association, the shift to staff operation of all activities but fund-raising occurs as rapidly as funds permit.

Even in fund-raising, a traditionally volunteer-run domain, staff members will take over management of special events, mail or telephone solicitations, membership campaigns, and large donor solicitation, although this last area usually depends on volunteers to do the actual peer solicitation.

During this stage, the industry or profession of an association continues to grow, and growth may be vigorous. However, sub-sets of the industry or profession may be forming and clamor-ing for recognition. The association may then face the problem of splinter groups threatening to break off and form new asso-ciations. In this event, associations' responses vary, ranging from trying to provide more services to accommodate the splinter groups to attempts to rein them in. These efforts place additional burdens on the staff.

In this third stage, the basic relationships between the staff and volunteer leaders take shape, and the fundamental culture of the organization solidifies. In volunteer-driven organiza-tions, the volunteers retain essential control through the officers, board, and committees. Volunteers retain authority to initiate and approve new activities and usually resist efforts by staff to assume more control. Volunteer control and direction are main-tained through a strong board and committee structure, an apparatus allowing the volunteers to formulate policy, tight control over the budget, and retention of a chief staff executive (CSE) who functions comfortably with the volunteers in charge.

In staff-driven associations, the staff take control in this third stage of development. Staff members propose policy decisions for approval by the board, initiate the development of new pro-grams, draw on the advice of volunteer committees while retaining the final say over what will be done, and develop expertise in the industry or profession which may exceed that of the volunteers.

Staff operation encourages volunteers to look to the staff for direction. In some cases, the volunteers actually wind up work-ing for the staff, particularly within the committee structure. Information shared with the board is controlled. The CSE is normally in close communication with the chief elected officer, perhaps daily, based on the chief elected officer's desire to be kept informed, but the communication is controlled on a need-to-know basis. While volunteer leaders continue to approve the annual budget, sign off on new activities, and receive reports from staff and volunteer committees, the staff has assumed basic control. A staff-driven culture predominates, at least until the volunteers rebel or there is a major crisis in the organization.

Many sources provide the impetus for the association to become basically staff- or volunteer-driven. Some of them develop in stage 2. In addition, a trade association often tends to become staff-driven because the representatives of the member companies or organizations are not personally committed to the association and lack the time to run it. Even when they are committed, management representatives who are used to delegating in their own organizations are quite comfortable delegating management of the association to paid staff.

Two important variants are trade associations composed of individual members (such as the National Association of Realtors) and those of companies run by their owners (such as the National Office Products Association). These trade associations tend to be more volunteer-driven than trade associations of organizational members, because the volunteer leaders may not be accustomed to delegating and may identify closely with the association.

Other important determinants of leadership mode include how the roles of the board and the CSE were initially set up and their evolution, the nature of problems that troubled the association in its early years and whether the volunteers stepped in to rescue the group, whether the CSE is from the profession or industry, and a host of other factors explored in detail in chapters 4 and 5. Finally, much depends on who the CSE is at this stage. If the incumbent is popular, effective, and wants to take control, the association is more likely to become staff-driven than if the CSE is uncertain, ineffective, unresponsive, or uncommunicative.

Once an association takes on a staff-driven or volunteer-driven character, the tendency is strong for it to remain that way. More than two-thirds of the trade and professional associations surveyed said that the history of volunteer or staff direction has remained fairly consistent over the long term. For philanthropic associations, the figure is 60 percent. Volunteer-driven trade and professional associations tend to be more stable in this respect than their staff-driven counterparts. In philanthropic associations, there is no difference in stability between staff- and volunteer-driven organizations.

Stage 4: Maturity

Associations take on a more or less permanent leadership mode as their industries, professions, or causes enter a mature stage, when growth is slowing down.

The growth rate of a mature industry is approximately equal to the GNP and is cyclical in nature. The industry's potential is reasonably well-known, and the primary markets may be approaching saturation. Companies are busy identifying and exploiting niches in the basic market and are exploring diversification, line extension, or gap-filling strategies. The number of competitors is generally stable or may even be declining slightly. Market shares have little volatility; firms with minor shares are unlikely to gain major shares. Entry into the industry is difficult either because of the large capital investment required or the extent of knowledge and experience needed to compete, or both. In the case of a service industry, most new competitors come out of older firms. Consolidations and failures act to keep the number of competitors relatively stable.

In a mature profession, the growth rate is equal to or some-what slower than growth in U.S. employment. Entry is difficult because of certification, licensure, and educational requirements. The self-image of the professionals is now sufficiently independent of the organizations that employ them that professionals shift organizations with ease. Depending on the nature of the profession and the support systems required, a significant number of professionals may function independently, for example, accountants, consultants, and marketers.

Professional subspecialization is significant at this stage, and, in some cases, the subspecialist group is larger and wields more clout than the original professional group. Ancillary people are now tolerated and may function under the direction of the professionals, although many ancillary people exert considerable effort to become more professional themselves. Indeed, ancillary, pre- or paraprofessional people may well be actively forming and establishing their own groups. The body of knowledge underpinning the profession is well developed and growing at the margins. Several journals serving the field may exist, and the professional association may publish more than one of them. Fee structures are well-known.

In the field of concern to the philanthropic association, most people who identify closely with the organization are known or have been reached through mailings and other promotional materials. Growth at the margins is offset by losses of older supporters. The potential for contributions has largely been attained, although the base could be enlarged significantly in the event of a major breakthrough or catastrophe or if the association discovers a more powerful marketing approach.

As the industry, profession, or concern matures, the association also continues its evolution by diversifying, developing new sources of income, adding new staff specialists, and generally spreading out. The thrust toward more and more staff operation continues, although in volunteer-driven associations, the basic initiatives and direction remain in the volunteers' hands.

As the staff take over more operational roles and people with specialized technical skills are added, some tension may develop around the question of who really is running the association and the degree to which the association should stray from its roots. Volunteers may sense a loss of control through yielding to more technically skilled staff in areas such as communications, meetings, publications, and government affairs. The officers and others among the volunteer leadership may complain about not being informed about all that is going on in the association.

The resulting tension is frequently expressed in the relationship between the chief elected officer and the CSE. Conflict between the two can take many forms and be worked out in numerous ways. The chief elected officer can assert authority, causing the CSE to back off. The CSE can conduct a running contest with each new chief elected officer, in which the CSE assumes authority when chief elected officers are more passive and retreats when they are more active. The board can call for a redefinition of each role, demanding written descriptions. Titles can be adjusted so that one or the other is named chief executive officer in an attempt to clarify authority. The possibilities are nearly endless for playing out this tension.

The point is that the authority and scope of the staff and the volunteer leaders shift as a result of an increasing workload, increasing technical content of the association's work, and the need to make longer-term commitments. The shift to staff control, however, is never made completely. The volunteers almost always hold on to some of the operational aspects and continue to perform some work that, theoretically, staff could do. Accommodating any shift in the roles and relationships of the CSE and chief elected officer is always a difficult task and one fraught with the potential for conflict.

Conflicts arise when the dynamic balance between volunteer and staff functions is upset or lost. Volunteers and staff leaders recognize trouble by way of many routes, but the most common are realizations that the volunteer leaders are not informed of decisions by the CSE, surprises about the association's finances, complaints from the upper-level staffers about lack of direction, or a sense that the CSE is too autocratic or too passive. Whatever the reason, leadership questions such as, ''Just who is running this place, anyhow?'' or ''Is anyone running this place?'' can signal problems for the CSE. If the executive, officers, and board cannot handle these conflicts, the CSE may be expelled and the association, in some ways, fractured.

The struggle over influence between the staff and volunteers is often masked or played out in a nobler and less threatening context. Two possibilities that work because they have inherent validity and importance are to relocate the association's headquarters and to alter the mission statement.

Stage 5: Aging

As a rule, associations age with their industries or professions. Aging industries are those experiencing a negative long-term growth rate. Market saturation has been reached, and little or no potential remains. The number of industry participants decreases, innovation is minimal, and entry is difficult. Rail box car manufacturing and shipbuilding in the United States are examples of aging industries.

For professions, the aging stage comes when employment is declining, people have little incentive to enter the profession, professional identity is blurred, the body of knowledge is static, and specialists and technicians have taken over many of the tasks that the profession once claimed as its own. Examples include leather chemists and general practitioners of medicine.

In a philanthropic association, a preventive to a chronic disease may have been discovered (although thousands afflicted with the problem may still be in need of services), or a social cause (such as saving whales) may have lost some of its energy because of legislation addressing the problem.

Aging for an association may come after a relatively brief existence or after many decades. Some associations have existed for well over 100 years and are still going strong. For example, the American Society of Civil Engineers was started in 1852, and the American Medical Association in 1847. Other associations have dissolved, been taken over, or suffered lingering deaths.

Many reasons exist for the aging and decline of an association. Some are associated with the aging and decline of the industry or profession. The Wool Hat Manufacturers Association, the American Association of Passenger Rate Men, the Cigarette Lighter Manufacturers Association, and the Religious Drygoods Association are defunct because their industries or professions are no longer viable.

Other associations, having been set up to solve a problem, lose their reason for existence when the problem is solved (although some turn to new problems and continue to function actively). Some associations started by a single individual whose energies kept it alive find no one left to continue the cause when the founder retires or dies. Still others begin as competitors to older and better established associations, perhaps by dissidents within the original parent organization. If the going gets rough, the members may give up the competition and return to the fold. Many associations merge with competing or complementary associations when the volunteer leaders of the two groups come to believe that the industry cannot support duplicate associations that serve much the same constituency and provide the same services.

An aging association may have a few active and very dedicated volunteers and a relatively entrenched staff, some of whom identify strongly with particular committee areas. Its staff have ceased to grow and, because of financial pressures, the association most likely has cut back on programs and services. Its orientation is one of maintaining, holding on, and, probably, denying its own decline. An astute leadership looks to transform the association by reorienting its focus and activities to parts of the industry or profession in earlier stages of the maturity cycle.

Variations on Maturation

Not all associations develop in synchrony with their environment, nor do all associations follow the same path. In some industries and professions, several associations may develop, each with its own subset of members. These associations may or may not eventually merge, depending on the view of the volunteers and on many other circumstances, such as the death or retirement of a CSE.

In the property-casualty insurance industry, for example, there are three large and viable trade associations: the American Insurance Association, representing many of the larger stock companies that sell through agents; the Alliance of American Insurers (Alliance), largely representing the mutual insurance companies, although more stock companies are joining; and the National Association of Independent Insurers (NAII), representing stock and mutual companies that refused to participate in the insurance rating bureaus which existed until the 1950s. Volunteer leaders of the three associations have attempted mergers over the years, but to date no merger has occurred because a significant number of member companies want to maintain separate organizations, even though operating three independent associations is probably more expensive than operating one consolidated group. Moreover, a significant number of large insurance companies decline to belong to any of the associations, a condition encouraged by the existence of three organizations. At this writing, a merger is again being considered, this time between the Alliance and NAII.

Some associations change their names, services, activities, and membership to keep pace with changes in the original industry or profession. The North American Telephone Association, established in 1970 and representing the interconnect industry, became in 1984 the North American Telecommunications Association. The Catholic Hospital Association became the Catholic Health Association and increased the scope of its activities in recognition that organized health care was taking hold outside of the traditional hospital setting. The association wanted to encompass as much of Catholic health care as possible rather than see affiliated groups splinter off.

The point is that specific factors in associations' maturation processes may look very different, one association from another, although each process follows a general pattern keyed to the growth and development of a particular industry or profession. In the early stages, an association will be volunteer-driven because it has no staff members or very few. As the staff grow and the organization develops, a pattern emerges indicating the degree to which the association is staff- or volunteer-driven and how long that mode will endure.

Crisis

For many associations, a financial or other crisis can set the stage for a significant, although usually temporary, shift in leadership mode. Whether the crisis is the result of a budget shortfall, perceived lack of leadership by the CSE, failed expectations, significant membership defection, or other causes, the volunteers will often move to take more control. In the process, the CSE is usually put on the defensive. In most cases, the organization reverts to its basic style once the crisis subsides. The CSE, however, may not survive.

The stage for a crisis that threatens the balance of volunteer-staff leadership is usually set much earlier. While the crisis may take many forms and often has a significant financial component, the context that calls the CSE's authority into doubt has typically developed over several years. There may have been a series of unanticipated budget deficits or unusually high staff turnover. The volunteer leaders may feel that they are not being given information needed to oversee the activities of the association. A series of chief elected officers may feel that the CSE does not treat them well. There may be a history of complaints from some segment of the membership that it is not being adequately heard or represented. Board members may feel that they are functioning like a rubber stamp on the CSE's proposals. There may be complaints from senior staff members that the association lacks direction from the top or that there is lax accountability within the structure.

Whatever the reasons, the stage is set for a crisis that becomes an occasion to question the CSE's ability to run the association. When this happens, the volunteers perceive a void in leadership and, accordingly, move in to fill it. At that point, the association becomes more volunteer-driven. Whether or not the CSE remains in the position depends on how he or she handles the situation.

In one staff-driven state trade association, the volunteer leaders felt for several years that the CSE was not sufficiently frank with elected officers about finances. While a majority of the board was content to let the CSE run things with a minimum of communication, the new president and president elect felt differently. They were concerned that major decisions were being made with insufficient volunteer input and were worried that new consulting and insurance programs initiated by the CSE exposed the association to great financial risk. When a cash flow squeeze forced the association to borrow money to meet operating expenses, the president took the opportunity to call for an investigation of the management and finances, a major initiative never before taken in the association's history.

The investigation revealed a significant lack of financial and managerial accountability. The study team noted that the association had taken on large health and liability insurance programs for its members with very little experience among the staff to manage such programs. The investigation resulted in dismissal of the association's controller, establishment of three new volunteer oversight committees, restructuring of the consulting service, and a requirement that the CSE be more forthcoming with the executive committee and board, consulting them in advance of committing resources to new activities. The CSE retained the support of the majority of the board and managed to hold on to his job, but his authority was considerably diminished for several years. With a change of volunteer leadership, the association is now back to being staff-driven, although with greater accountability by the CSE to volunteer leaders.

In this case, an undercurrent of dissatisfaction erupted due to a perceived financial crisis. Had the CSE been more forthright with the volunteer leadership, particularly about the realities of the association's cash flow, the situation may never have developed into a crisis. However, when the volunteer leaders declared a crisis, they moved in and took greater control.

Chapter 4

Characteristics of the Leadership Modes

T his chapter explores those characteristics of associations which directly correlate with a staff-driven or volunteer-driven leadership mode, as well as those which might be expected to correlate but do not.* The discussion provides a base for strategies that a chief staff executive (CSE) might employ to shift the leadership mode of the association.

Correlating Factors

Association Type

The most obvious factor affecting a volunteer- and staff-driven leadership mode is the type of association, whether trade, professional, or philanthropic. In general, trade associations with corporate or organizational members are the most staff-driven, and health-oriented philanthropic associations are the least (table 1). All associations, but particularly professional

---

*The correlations are based on survey responses from 234 trade and professional associations and 184 philanthropic health and social service or social welfare associations, supplemented by extensive interviews with chief staff executives (CSEs) and chief elected officers. The CSEs surveyed estimated the degree to which their organizations were staff- or volunteer-driven, and these estimates were checked against other data on each association to assess their validity. In some cases the sample size for a subset of the respondents was too small to yield reliable information, and no conclusions were drawn.

Table 1

Prevalence of Leadership Modes by Association Type, 1988 and 1978*

Type of Association	1988			1978		
	Staff-Driven	Volunteer-Driven	Balanced	Staff-Driven	Volunteer-Driven	Balanced
Trade associations						
corporate members	60%	7%	33%	44%	29%	27%
individual members	44	18	38	37	33	30
Professional societies	41	15	44	18	59	23
Philanthropic						
social welfare or social service	42	4	54	33	29	38
health	40	6	54	34	32	34

*Data are based on the opinions of chief staff executives. In 1988, the average staff size for the trade and professional associations was 16.7 people, with a median of 7.8; for philanthropic associations, the average staff size was 35.4 people, with a median of 19.0.

societies and corporate trade associations, have become more staff-driven over the past decade (table 2). The greatest change toward the staff-driven mode has taken place in professional, scientific, and engineering societies. Trade associations with corporate members, already the most staff-driven, became even more so during the ten-year period from 1978 to 1988. Philanthropic associations, predominately staff-driven a decade ago, shifted the least, indicating a more stable leadership mode than their trade and professional counterparts.

What has happened over the past ten years to make associations more staff-driven? The primary causes seem to be staff professionalization and organizational growth and diversification. CSEs of all kinds of associations said that a more professional staff is the principal reason behind the change: 80 percent of the trade associations, 73 percent of the professional societies,

Table 2

Chief Staff Executives' Ratings of Leadership Modes in Their Associations

Type of Association	Average Rating*		Percentage Change
	1978	1988	1978 to 1988
Trade associations			
corporate members	5.38	6.71	24.7%
individual members	4.98	5.83	17.1
Professional societies	3.59	5.64	57.1
Philanthropic associations			
social service or social welfare	5.02	5.73	14.1
health	5.03	5.44	8.2

*A rating of 0 indicates that an association is totally volunteer-driven and of 9, totally staff-driven.

97 percent of the philanthropic social welfare associations, and 88 percent of the philanthropic health associations gave staff professionalism as a significant factor. The change in professionalism is particularly noticeable at the regional, state, and local levels.

Diversification and growth, too, play a major role. CSEs said that their organizations are now engaged in more technical activities requiring staff direction than a decade ago. Almost half of the trade and professional associations indicated that an increase in nondues income has been a factor in the shift. Even philanthropic associations cited increased nondues and non-contribution-based income as a significant cause in becoming more staff-driven.

Sheer growth was mentioned by many executives as a major impetus for the shift, although, paradoxically, the size of associations does not correlate with a staff-driven or volunteer-driven leadership mode. So, it seems to be the rate of growth rather than absolute size that helps to determine whether an association shifts.

Why are proportionately more trade associations than professional and scientific societies staff-driven? Three main reasons came to light. First, CSEs and volunteer leaders of trade associations reported that their volunteers frequently do not have the time required to run the association. Volunteer leaders of professional societies, by way of contrast, seem to have more time available, perhaps because so many of them are from academia. Time volunteered by members of professional societies is not necessarily time off from their work. For academics, in particular, active participation in a professional society may directly advance their status and compensation and is seen as an important part of their jobs.

A second reason is the difference in work styles and personal investments between businesspeople and professionals. Business leaders value efficiency and are accustomed to delegating, whereas professionals and scientists frequently engage in projects where there is little delegation and efficiency is of secondary importance. A professional society often engages in activities, such as publishing, certification, and professional recognition, that directly affect the professional's income, status, or ability to practice. In short, professionals are more likely to benefit directly from participation in their associations. Hence, these members may be reluctant to turn over the control and direction of these activities to the paid staff.

The third reason is the members' degree of expertise. In a professional society, proportionately more association activities are devoted to matters that the members readily understand, such as publications, education, and professional standards. Consequently, they may feel quite competent to participate and, indeed, may be more competent than professional staff. In trade associations more activity is devoted to lobbying, legal affairs, and the collection of industry statistics, all of which require technical expertise beyond the capabilities or interest of most volunteer leaders.

In business-based trade associations comprising individual members (real estate brokers, insurance agents, and so forth), the tendency to be staff-driven is strong but not as pronounced as in trade associations with corporate or organizational members. The individual members of these trade groups usually own their own businesses or are independent contractors and agents. While they may have difficulty scheduling time to participate actively in association affairs and while government affairs may be the primary activity, these members still feel a strong sense of ownership. Participation enables them to make useful business contacts and affects their status in the field. In these respects, then, these trade associations are similar to professional associations.

Philanthropic associations have remained relatively stable in their leadership mode compared with other associations. Why? The reason may lie in their focus—on a cause, problem, or movement—generally apart from the direct economic or professional concerns of the members. Philanthropic associations were largely staff-driven ten years ago and have stayed that way, with the volunteer leaders preferring to let the professional staffs direct and operate the organizations, while reserving some pockets for substantial volunteer input, particularly in fund-raising.

Growth

Three indexes of association growth are the number of members, income, and number of full-time staff. Along most of these measures, staff-driven associations have outperformed volunteer-driven associations during the decade 1978 to 1988 (table 3).

The percentage growth in *members* over the past ten years was significantly higher among the staff-driven associations surveyed than the volunteer-driven associations. The average staff-driven trade and professional association grew 45 percent, while the average volunteer-driven association grew 10 percent.

For trade and professional organizations, the *income* of the average staff-driven association surveyed grew 91 percent over the 1978 to 1988 period, while income of the average volunteer-driven association grew 50 percent. In philanthropic associations, income of the average staff-driven organization grew 77 percent and that of the average volunteer-driven association 72 percent.

Table 3

Comparisons of Growth Between Staff-Driven and Volunteer-Driven Associations, 1978 to 1988

Type of Association	Growth from 1978 to 1988		
	Members	Income	Staff
Trade and professional			
staff-driven	45%	91%	32%
volunteer-driven	10	50	38
Philanthropic			
staff-driven	na*	77	35
volunteer-driven	na*	72	37

*Membership figures for philanthropic associations are not very meaningful, since some members comprise contributors and others do not. Many philanthropic associations do not have members as such.

The final measure of recorded growth is the increase in number of *full-time staff.* According to that measure, during the past ten years, staff-driven trade and professional associations grew on average 32 percent, while volunteer-driven associations grew 38 percent. For philanthropic associations, staff-driven organizations grew 35 percent and volunteer-driven associations 34 percent.

The Chief Staff Executive as CEO

The acronym *CEO,* chief executive officer, derives from a corporate context and refers to the person in charge who is the final authority and the principal decision maker and policy setter in an organization.

Staff-driven associations designate their chief staff executives as CEOs more often than volunteer-driven associations. The chief staff executives of trade and professional associations are designated CEOs in 35 percent of those which are staff-driven and in 21 percent of those which are volunteer-driven. In philanthropic associations, the chief staff executive is designated CEO in 36 percent of the staff-driven organizations and in 27 percent of the volunteer-driven organizations. These differences, while not great, seem to reflect the greater authority accorded the staff in staff-driven organizations.

The designation can be misleading, however, because in some associations, the CEO title is assigned to the position that does not drive the organization. In volunteer-driven associations, the chief staff executive is called the CEO in about 25 percent of the cases, and in staff-driven associations, the chief elected officer is designated the CEO in 14 percent of the cases.

In slightly more than half of the associations surveyed, no individual is designated as CEO (trade and professional, 56 percent; philanthropic, 50 percent). Although the term is coming into more common use among associations, the majority are still reluctant to name one position as CEO. The reality of the functioning and structure of associations tends to support the choice not to designate a CEO.

In a business, the CEO typically has great power in determining direction and policy. The purposes and organization of an association, however, are quite different from those of a business. Businesses exist to make a profit and to find and create customers for their products and services. Associations exist to empower the members, to reduce members' isolation, and to provide a sense of identity to individuals and organizations. Associations also provide a wide range of services in such areas as insurance, information, and surveys, but these services are typically not priced to maximize profits, nor is the expectation of profit necessarily the reason for offering the services. Further, there may be little direct competition for these services from other associations or from businesses.

In a business, owners, managers, and workers usually can agree on the general purpose or, at least, the general measure of performance—profit—even though they may differ greatly on how to accomplish that purpose. In an association, no such basic starting point exists, even for fee-based services.[11] The purposes of the association are whatever its leaders say they are. Frequently, the basic purposes must be reinvented or restated to stay in tune with the conditions of the industry, profession, or cause that binds the membership. Thus, an association may start with a mission of bringing together the members for mutual support and comradeship and, then, in mid-course, change the mission to achieving preeminence for the industry or profession.

In an association, one person can rarely speak for the interests of all members in defining the purposes and setting direction. Accordingly, a board of directors or trustees (a representative group rather than an individual) usually sets the basic policy and direction of the association. This group—the governing board—carries out the function of the chief executive in most associations. Therefore, although the chief staff executive may be designated as CEO, in practice the CEO function is a collective one exercised by the board. In many cases, it is the executive committee that actually performs the decision-making function of CEO, but its authority to do so is delegated by the entire board.

The message for chief staff executives is to take the title *CEO* with a large grain of salt; CEO in the association community does not carry the same meaning as in the business world. To the person considering the job of chief staff executive, the title *CEO* can be a tip-off that the association is run more by staff than volunteers. What the title does not imply is that the CEO has the power to run the association like a business.

Voting Status

CSEs are usually not voting members of their boards. Only 14 percent of the trade and professional associations and 10 percent of the philanthropic associations reported that CSEs held a vote on the board.

The CSEs of staff-driven trade and professional associations are more likely to have a board vote (21 percent) than their counterparts in volunteer-driven associations (6 percent). In philanthropic associations, twice as many CSEs of volunteer-driven groups reported that they are voting members of the board than of staff-driven groups; in neither case was the number greater than 20 percent. There are no amplifying data to explain why this is so.

In most associations, board members feel more comfortable if the CSE is not a voting member. This enables the board to more freely direct the CSE, meet in executive session, and evaluate the CSE's performance. Although few boards actually conduct a formal evaluation process, nearly all like to have that option.

Employment Contracts

Employment contracts often spell out the roles and responsibilities of the CSE, compensation, duration of the contract, and processes for termination. In formulating the contract, volunteer leaders must assess the degree to which the CSE will direct the staff, formulate policy, interact with the board, and be a spokesperson.

The use of employment contracts is becoming more prevalent in associations to protect the executive and the board, and both are now requesting them. This trend may stem from the gradual emergence of association management as a profession.

The use of employment contracts differs between staff- and volunteer-driven organizations. Among trade and professional associations, more staff-driven associations (55 percent) than volunteer-driven associations (42 percent) have employment contracts with their CSEs. Philanthropic associations generally use employment contracts less frequently and the proportions between staff- and volunteer-driven organizations are reversed: 25 percent of the staff-driven philanthropic associations have employment contracts with the CSE, compared with 35 percent of the volunteer-driven organizations.

Accountability

Among all associations, the CSE reports directly to the board or executive committee about two-thirds of the time; the remaining percentage reports first to the chief elected officer and then to the board. In volunteer-driven trade and professional associations, the CSE reports directly to the chief elected officer more often (36 percent) than in staff-driven associations (25 percent). The same trend is borne out in philanthropic associations. The CSE's reporting to the chief elected officer is indicative of a volunteer-driven mode; reporting to the board or executive committee is consistent with a staff-driven mode.

Authority over Personnel and Spending

In personnel and finances, the CSEs of staff-driven associations have greater latitude and authority than their counterparts in volunteer-driven associations. The CSE hires, fires, and promotes staff without the approval of volunteer leaders in 51 percent of the staff-driven trade and professional associations and 58 percent of the staff-driven philanthropic associations. Among volunteer-driven associations, the figures are 34 percent and 35 percent, respectively. In the remainder of cases, CSEs report that, although they have authority to act independently, they normally seek the approval of volunteer leaders before making moves among senior staff. A very small percentage report that volunteer leaders must approve personnel actions below the senior staff ranks.

In the budgetary area, the results are similar. The CSEs of staff-driven associations have more latitude to exceed the budget and shift expenditures among line items than those of volunteer-driven associations. In staff-driven trade and professional associations, 10 percent of the CSEs report that they may not exceed budgeted line items without approval from the board, compared with 22 percent in volunteer-driven associations. In philanthropic associations, the results are roughly comparable: 13 percent of the CSEs in staff-driven organizations and 32 percent in volunteer-driven organizations may not exceed budgeted line items without first seeking approval from the board or executive committee.

In many cases, the CSE's actual authority is greater than what he or she exercises. Many CSEs report that they have authority to exceed the budget and to shift expenditures but, as a practical matter, do not without first checking with the volunteer leadership.

Chief Elected Officers: Time Spent on Association Business

Chief elected officers of volunteer-driven trade or professional associations spend on average 38 percent of their time (almost two days a week) on association business, compared with their counterparts in staff-driven associations, who spend an average of 25 percent. The picture for philanthropic associations differs in degree. The chief elected officers of volunteer-driven philanthropic associations spend an average of 18 percent of their time (about one day a week) on association business; in staff-driven philanthropic associations, the average is 15 percent.

There is essentially no difference in the time spent by officers of trade and professional associations whether they serve a national association or a state or local association, despite an assumption that the physical proximity of the association to the officeholder would affect the amount of time spent in volunteering. While these officers all report spending an average of 29 percent of their time on association business, how they spend the time may be quite different. It is entirely possible, for example, that national-level chief elected officers spend their time at extended meetings and in traveling, while state and local chief elected officers spend more time in the association office.

In philanthropic associations, the picture is even more surprising. The amount of time that chief elected officers of national associations spend on volunteer work (23 percent) is almost double that spent by their counterparts at the state and local levels (13 percent). Perhaps the greater prestige and visibility of a national-level office helps to explain the difference, as well as how the time is spent.

Contested Elections

The elections of chief elected officers are more likely to be contested in volunteer-driven associations than in staff-driven associations. Among volunteer-driven trade and professional associations, 47 percent had experienced contested elections for the chief elected officer; among staff-driven associations, 31 percent.

These findings again reflect the fact that professional societies tend to be more volunteer-driven than trade associations. Professional societies, because of their typically large individual memberships, are twice as likely to have contested elections for the chief elected position (58 percent) than trade associations with corporate or organizational members (27 percent). About one-third of trade associations with individual members have had contested elections.

Among philanthropic groups, 35 percent of the volunteer-driven associations have had contested elections for chief elected officers, compared with 19 percent of the staff-driven associations.

Despite the skewing of contested elections toward individual membership associations, one may speculate that contested elections spur the nominees to specify what they would do as the chief elected officer, if not to the entire membership, then to the volunteer leadership. By stating their ideas for the association, they help to create a context within which the association will function. The intentions may embody no more than a single new activity or boosting membership but, if translated into action, represent volunteer direction of part of the association's agenda. It is not surprising, therefore, that volunteer-driven associations have more contested elections than staff-driven organizations.

Gender

In trade and professional associations, the gender of the CSE and chief elected officer correlates with the leadership mode; in philanthropic associations, it does not. Slightly more than 40 percent of the CSEs of volunteer-driven trade and professional associations are women, compared with slightly more than 20 percent in staff-driven associations. Among chief elected officers, the figures are 21 percent and 9 percent, respectively. As a basis for comparison, in all trade and professional associations surveyed (national, state, and local), about 25 percent of the CSEs and 13 percent of the chief elected officers are women.

In philanthropic associations, women comprise 37 percent of the CSEs, whether the group is staff- or volunteer-driven, and slightly more than 25 percent of the chief elected officers.

Board Size

A comparison of the size of governing boards of trade and professional associations shows that the boards of volunteer-driven associations are, on average, 18 percent larger than those of staff-driven associations. The median size of boards in volunteer-driven associations is 18.25 members and in staff-driven associations, 15.5 members. Larger boards in volunteer-driven associations may reflect emphasis on including as many elements of the membership as possible, whereas in a staff-driven association, the emphasis may be on greater efficiency.

The same relationship holds for the boards of philanthropic associations. The median board size for a volunteer-driven association is 35.9 members and for a staff-driven association, 31.4 members.

Delegate Assemblies

Delegate assemblies are large bodies (average size, 150 people) that usually meet once a year. Overall, 51 percent of philanthropic associations and 28 percent of trade and professional associations have such bodies. Individual member associations, trade and professional, have delegate assemblies more often than associations with corporate or organizational members.

Delegate assemblies often wield considerable power in selecting members of the board, passing resolutions, and approving budgets. These decisions guide and provide a framework for activities, pushing the association toward the volunteer-driven mode.

Volunteer-driven associations are much more likely to have delegate assemblies than staff-driven associations. Forty-three percent of volunteer-driven professional and trade associations have such assemblies, compared with 24 percent of staff-driven associations; 71 percent of volunteer-driven philanthropic associations have delegate assemblies, compared with 43 percent of staff-driven organizations.

Executive Committees

Executive committees are responsible for overseeing the association's administration and for making policy decisions between meetings of the board. Among the organizations surveyed, the typical executive committee comprises eight to ten members elected or appointed for two-year terms and meets bimonthly with the CSE to review operations and performance against budget and to address situations needing volunteer decisions.

The vast majority of associations of all kinds have executive committees, but the incidence differs among volunteer-driven and staff-driven trade and professional associations, with 85 percent of volunteer-driven groups having executive committees and 74 percent of staff-driven associations having executive committees.

Among philanthropic associations, there is no difference in the incidence of executive committees between staff- and volunteer-driven organizations. Eighty-eight percent of both types of groups have executive committees.

Counterpart Committees

Counterpart committees are composed of volunteers who oversee or serve as advisors in areas of the association where full-time staff are also involved. These areas could include education, conventions and meetings, standards, member services, publications, or many other activities.

Among trade and professional associations that are volunteer-driven, 45 percent report counterpart volunteer committees to most or all staff departments; in staff-driven trade and professional associations, the figure is 32 percent. Among philanthropic associations, 70 percent of the volunteer-driven organizations report that most or all staff departments have corresponding volunteer committees, compared with 51 percent of staff-driven organizations.

The members and chair of a counterpart committee usually develop an understanding of the workings of a staff department and influence its operation. If the committee has a say in the department's budget, either by advocating or by actually determining the annual budget requests, then its influence over the functioning of the department can be considerable.

In cases where the committee chair is also a board or executive committee member, that person's advocacy on program and budget matters can undercut the CSE's ability to manage the department.

The role of counterpart committees is significant when assessing the differences between a staff- and a volunteer-driven association. Among volunteer-driven trade and professional associations with counterpart committees, 38 percent report that committees direct staff activities. Of staff-driven trade and professional associations, 19 percent report committee direction of staff. Among philanthropic associations, 65 percent of volunteer-driven groups with counterpart committees report that committees direct staff activities, and 16 percent of staff-driven groups so report.

Personal interviews with CSEs and their volunteer leaders point up the importance of the relationship between committees and staff in determining whether an association is volunteer- or staff-driven. When committees direct the staff, the association is likely to be volunteer-driven. When committees advise the staff, the association is more likely to be staff-driven.

Reimbursement of Expenses

Committee members' expenses are reimbursed more often in volunteer-driven associations than in staff-driven associations, whether trade, professional, or philanthropic. Fifty-five percent of volunteer-driven trade and professional associations and 62 percent of volunteer-driven philanthropic associations reimburse expenses. It is unclear whether and to what extent reimbursement contributes to an association's being volunteer-driven, is a result of being volunteer-driven, or is a combination of both.

Tenure of Senior Staff

On average, the senior staff of staff-driven associations serve 15 percent longer (a full year) than staff of volunteer-driven associations. In staff-driven trade and professional associations, senior staff serve an average of 6.7 years and in volunteer-driven associations, an average of 5.9 years. In philanthropic associations, they serve 7.4 years in staff-driven and 6.4 years in volunteer-driven groups.

These findings are consistent with what one would expect from the leadership modes. Volunteers defer more to senior, experienced staff, because of their expertise, than to less experienced staff. Senior staffs of staff-driven associations may find that their working situations are more stable than those of their volunteer-driven counterparts, that they have more control over situations, and that they are less subject to capricious firings by volunteers.

Income-Generating Services

Association services and products are purchased primarily by the members or, in the cases of advertising and exhibits, by vendors. Many services and products are technical, for example, information services, insurance, and exhibit sales. Because the members may not have the specialized know-how required, producing these services is not amenable to substantial member input and direction. Accordingly, it was hypothesized that services would be largely staff-driven and that a high proportion of staff-driven services in the total mix of association activities would most often yield a staff-driven association.

Are income-producing services more staff-driven than associations as a whole? Yes, although the data do not make clear how much the leadership mode of services influences the overall leadership mode of the association. Staff-driven associations ranked their income-generating services the same as the associations as a whole—7.89, with 9 being totally staff-driven. Volunteer-driven associations rated their income-generating services as 4.15, a ranking indicating that these are more staff-driven than the associations overall (2.12).

The survey results also suggest that philanthropic associations deriving significant income from the sale of traditional products and services (such as publications, education, meetings, and exhibit services) are more staff-driven. In staff-driven philanthropic associations, an average of 33 percent of total revenue derives from services and products; in volunteer-driven philanthropic associations, 20 percent.

The results for trade and professional associations, however, are less supportive of the hypothesis that more income from products and services means a more staff-driven association. Staff-driven trade and professional associations derive an average of 42 percent of their total income from services and products, compared with 48 percent in volunteer-driven associations.

To add to the confusion, when asked why their associations are more staff-driven today than ten years ago, 45 percent of trade and professional executives and 31 percent of philanthropic executives cited increases in nondues income.

One must conclude, therefore, that if an association increases the percentage of its income from services and products, the entire association tends to become more staff-driven, although the extent of the shift is impossible to predict.

Strategic Planning

The majority of the associations surveyed have engaged in strategic planning. Among trade and professional associations, 61 percent of the volunteer-driven organizations reported formal strategic planning during the past five years, and among staff-driven associations, 69 percent have done so. Among philanthropic associations, the figures are 27 percent of volunteer-driven and 22 percent of staff-driven groups.

Strategic planning can be a way to increase the influence of volunteers and staff alike (also see chapter 9). A majority of volunteer-driven associations of all kinds reported that strategic planning increased the influence of volunteers, and a majority of staff-driven associations reported that strategic planning increased the influence of staff.

Noncorrelating Factors

Scope

The scope of an association—whether international, national, regional, state, or local—seems to make little difference in the extent to which it is staff- or volunteer-driven (table 4). Put another way, the geographic proximity of the members to the association's headquarters does not seem to be a significant factor in leadership mode. In fact, local associations are slightly more staff-driven than state or national associations. The increased possibilities that proximity affords for volunteers' direct interaction with staff and unplanned, drop-by interventions do not seem to translate into greater volunteer direction.

Table 4

Relationship of Geographic Scope to Leadership Mode

Scope	Volunteer-Driven	Staff-Driven
Trade and professional associations		
international, national	15%	47%
state	14	45
local	17	58
Philanthropic associations		
international, national	9	36
state	20	34
local	16	37

Staff Size

The survey encompassed associations of all staff sizes, ranging from one to more than 1,000. Survey results do not suggest that size correlates with leadership mode.

The volunteer-driven trade and professional associations average 17.76 staff members (median, 6.79) and have average budgets of $1.9 million (median, $0.9 million). Staff-driven trade and professional associations are slightly smaller, with an average of 16.95 staff members (median, 7.32) and average budgets of $1.6 million (median, $0.65 million).

For philanthropic associations, the picture is mixed, but again, the differences are not great. The volunteer-driven philanthropic associations average 25.60 staff members (median, 15.63) and budgets of $1.9 million (median, $1.5 million). The average staff-driven philanthropic association includes 31.03 staff members (median, 14.17) and a budget of $2.0 million (median, $0.8 million).

One would expect staff size to bear some correlation to leadership mode, particularly since associations tend to become more staff-driven during their early to middle stages of growth. The reason for the discrepancy may be that, although associations may shift from volunteer to staff operation, the initiative and direction, once established, remain with the volunteers. Moreover, even though the leadership mode of many volunteer-driven associations may shift as they grow one or two points away from the volunteer-driven end of the scale, they still rank as volunteer-driven organizations.

Tenure of the Chief Staff Executive

Although CSEs with long tenure in their positions might be expected more heavily to influence the direction of the organization than those with shorter lengths of service, there was no significant difference in tenure between volunteer-driven and staff-driven associations. The CSEs of trade and professional associations had an average length of service of six years, with executives of staff-driven associations serving a few months longer, on average, than those of volunteer-driven associations. In philanthropic associations, the average was eight years, with the volunteer-driven association executive serving slightly longer.

CAE Designation

Among the associations surveyed there was little variation in the percentage of executives who had earned or were working on earning the Certified Association Executive (CAE) designation. Seventeen percent of the trade and professional association executives and 4 percent of the philanthropic association executives reported having their CAE designation. Another 15 percent and 14 percent, respectively, said they are working on it. The difference between volunteer- and staff-driven associations was negligible.

Income of the Chief Staff Executive

In staff- and volunteer-driven associations of all types, the income of the CSE is, on average, lower than that of the average board member. In only 22 percent of the trade and professional associations and 15 percent of the philanthropic associations was the income of the CSE estimated to be higher. The difference between staff-driven and volunteer-driven associations was negligible.

Previous Affiliation of the Chief Staff Executive

There are no significant differences between staff-driven and volunteer-driven associations regarding the previous affiliation of the CSE. In trade and professional associations, approximately 50 percent of the CSEs came from the industry or profession, 25 percent from another association in a different industry or profession, and 25 percent from other arenas, including government service as an elected or appointed official or a congressional staffer.

In philanthropic associations, approximately 50 percent of the CSEs were previously with the association in another permanent capacity, 10 percent with the organization in a volunteer capacity, and 40 percent from outside the organization. The only noticeable difference is that more executives in volunteer-driven associations than in staff-driven associations were previously volunteers (15 percent compared with 6 percent).

Chapter 5

Leadership Modes by Type of Association

This chapter focuses on the leadership modes by type of association. For the purposes of analysis, associations are broken into five categories, including trade associations, corporate members; trade associations, individual members;* professional societies; philanthropic health associations; and philanthropic social welfare or social service associations.

One of the principal findings to emerge from the study is that trade associations are significantly more staff-driven than other associations, and professional societies are among the least staff-driven of associations. The survey results also indicate that association executives of all types judge their organizations to be more staff-driven than volunteer-driven (see table 1), and the trend is for associations to become more staff-driven over time. This chapter sheds light on the characteristics of the various types of organizations and their members that give them a propensity to be staff-driven or volunteer-driven, or to function with a balanced influence of staff and volunteers.

Trade Associations, Corporate Members

A trade association offers volunteers a way to associate with other industry representatives, learn from one another, and agree on industry-wide policy for expression in the legislative and regulatory arenas.

---

*Trade associations with individual members comprise business-based associations whose members are individuals engaged in a trade or a business pursuit. Examples include the National Association of Realtors and the National Association for Hospital Development.

In some industries, member companies are primarily publicly held corporations with professional managers as the chief executive officers. These executives may head organizations that dwarf the industry association in revenues, staff, and technical talent.

Trade associations with large corporate members tend to be more staff-driven than other types of associations for several reasons. First, volunteers in these associations represent a company or organization rather than themselves. The principal volunteer serving on the association's board is most often the chief executive officer or head of a line of business of the member organization. Lower-level executives may serve on the association's committees dealing with particular facets of the industry.

The chief executive officers of these member companies are used to delegating responsibility. They involve themselves in matters of corporate strategy and decisions affecting the organization as a whole; the analyses underlying decisions are performed by subordinates. This characteristic tends to carry over into the executive's participation in the association. Trade association staff members are looked on as extensions of the company staff in that they have technical expertise that the chief executive officer does not need to emulate. The work of the association, therefore, is delegated to the association staff, with the member representative on the board reacting to issues and decision requirements rather than initiating them. The initiatives, in many cases, come from staff, either directly or via committees reporting to the board.

A second reason that trade associations with corporate members tend to be staff-driven is the amount of time member company representatives have to give to the association. The propensity to delegate receives reinforcement from the fact that professional managers and chief executive officers often have neither the time nor the energy to run the association as a chief elected officer. On average, they report that they are not as able as owner-managers to take time off from work to run the association, even on a half-time basis. If the association is running smoothly, they are content to attend or chair quarterly or semi-annual board meetings, hear reports, vote, and leave.

Third, industry representatives may want to be involved only in selected activities of the association. Some volunteers, for example, are principally concerned about and active in legislative and regulatory affairs. With few exceptions, however (notably the chief elected officer and members of the board and executive or finance committees), the principal volunteers in a trade association comprising large companies are much less concerned about the details of running the association. The volunteers who are involved in more technical activities, such as developing data on the industry, the technical aspects of putting out the association's publications, and relationships with other associations, generally are lower-level executives in member companies and are not encouraged to run association affairs. Rather, they advise the staff and carry out their technical deliberations as required. Consequently, most of the actual operation of the association is left to staff.

Fourth, for many chief executive officers of companies, trade associations are a peripheral interest to the affairs of their own organizations. Nevertheless, associations are useful; they handle certain data collecting and lobbying functions better than the individual companies and perform other functions, such as convening the industry, that are impossible for the individual companies. So, the chief executive officer gives time as needed but seldom enough to run the association.

Finally, the principal activities of trade associations with corporate members lend themselves to the staff-driven mode. For example, government affairs at national and state levels—often a top priority—are frequently technical in nature, focus on regulation as well as legislation, require keeping abreast of massive amounts of information, and necessitate taking quick action. Conducting these functions well requires a skilled, full-time professional staff. While volunteers can provide general oversight and be very effective in testifying and contacting legislators, their work must be coordinated, guided, and backed by staff. For these reasons, trade associations with corporate members tend to be more staff-driven than trade associations with individual members or professional societies.

As with any generalization, there are exceptions. Trade associations with members comprising small companies, while largely staff-driven, tend to involve volunteers more in the day-to-day direction. Volunteer leaders from owner-managed companies (such as printing firms, restaurants, construction firms, wholesale distribution firms, and office supply dealers) usually identify more closely and personally with their companies than the professional managers of large public companies. They may, thus, feel more obligated to serve their industries by participation in the association. In such cases, association leadership is seen as a mark of industry recognition and status.

Furthermore, the association can offer owners of small enterprises some measure of protection from or control over economic and government forces that affect their businesses. The association's legislative and government affairs function, in particular, can effect real financial savings through changes in tax, labor, safety, waste disposal, and reporting laws. In addition, the association may offer valuable education, insurance, and other services that are not readily available elsewhere. Unlike members representing large firms, those representing small firms do not as easily delegate control of such an important organization to professional managers, for its activities cut too closely to home.

Listed next are some of the more significant survey results about trade associations with corporate members.

- Only 27 percent have contested elections for their officers, compared with 34 percent for trade associations with individual members and 58 percent for professional societies.

- Chief elected officers of these trade associations spend 25 percent of their time on association business, compared with 33 percent spent by their professional association counterparts.

- In 19 percent of these trade associations (compared with 13 percent in professional societies), the CSE is directly accountable to the board or executive committee, rather than to the chief elected officer, and is a voting member of the board.

- CSEs of these trade associations more frequently seek approval from the volunteer leadership before making personnel moves among the senior staff, even though they possess the authority to take such actions alone. Their spending authority to shift expenditures among budgeted line items and to exceed overall budgets is essentially the same as in other types of associations.

- More so than other types of associations, these trade associations have a committee structure that does not parallel the staff structure. Fully 40 percent of these trade associations report having no counterpart volunteer committees, compared with 26 percent of trade associations with individual members and 21 percent of professional societies.

- These trade associations infrequently experience change in their leadership mode: More than 75 percent of their CSEs reported a fairly consistent long-term direction.

Trade Associations, Individual Members

In many trade associations, members join as individuals, although their businesses in almost all cases pay their dues. The focus of the association is primarily on the industry and its needs, and secondarily on the advancement of the individual member, mainly through education. One of the largest individual member trade associations is the National Association of Realtors (NAR), totaling more than 750,000 members who represent approximately 150,000 firms. Affiliated with the national are 50 state associations and more than 1,700 local Realtor boards, each of which is a separate association and most of which have paid staffs. Other examples of trade associations with individual members include agricultural commodity associations; associations of functional specialists in corporations, such as risk managers and comptrollers; and independent contractors of various kinds.

While staff-driven when taken collectively, trade associations with individual members are less so than trade associations with corporate members, averaging 5.82 on a scale of 0 to 9 (with 0 being totally volunteer-driven and 9 totally staff-driven), compared with a 6.59 average for corporate trade groups.

One inference for why this is so is that individual members, like the owners of small- and medium-sized businesses, identify more personally with their businesses and industries and therefore take a greater interest in their associations' affairs. They also have less experience working within bureaucratic organizations than professional managers. One may also infer that individual members look to their trade association for a variety of important services, including education, information on industry trends and developments, insurance, and legislative and regulatory advocacy. Because these services are seen as directly affecting their livelihood, individual members are reluctant to turn over control to staff.

Listed next are survey results that distinguish trade associations with individual membership from other types of associations with respect to leadership mode.

- A higher proportion, 43 percent, have delegate assemblies than other types of associations (30 percent for professional societies and 18 percent for trade associations with corporate members). The presence of a delegate assembly generally correlates with the volunteer-driven mode. Their governing boards are smaller than those of other associations, averaging 17 members, compared with an average of 22 members for other trade associations and professional societies.

- Unlike professional societies, most do not have contested elections for officers. Of the CSEs of these trade associations surveyed, 34 percent reported contested elections for their officers, compared with 58 percent for professional societies.

- The chief elected officers are more often women (20 percent) than in other types of associations (16 percent in professional societies and 6 percent in trade associations with corporate members).

- The CSE is more often designated the CEO (35 percent) than in trade associations with corporate members (25 percent) or professional societies (23 percent).

Professional Societies

Almost all professional societies (including engineering and scientific societies) are individual member organizations. Membership may range from the hundreds of thousands of individuals in some national societies, such as the Institute of Electrical and Electronic Engineers, American Medical Association, and American Bar Association, to a few hundred individuals in some state or local societies. Like the owners of small enterprises who identify closely with their industries, the members of professional societies gain much of their identity from their profession.

The volunteer leaders of a professional society are usually elected by the members, sometimes at large and sometimes from local chapters or regional groupings. Leaders may also be appointed or elected from subdisciplines or special interest groups within the profession. Committee chairs are usually appointed by the chief elected officer.

The professional society normally performs functions and services that at least some members feel are vital to their careers. The journals of academic societies are primary vehicles for publishing research papers that lead to professional advancement, for providing valuable technical information to members, and for disseminating information on the association itself. Meetings of the society are a prime means of presenting new technical information and for establishing important contacts. Continuing education programs may be essential to retaining professional certification. On occasion, government affairs activities may make a real financial or professional difference to the members. For those members active in its affairs, the association is extremely important. Decisions and activities of the association can directly affect their livelihood, status, and future. It is all too important to turn over completely to paid staff.

The result is that, in many professional societies, the volunteers are actively involved in and direct the work of the organization. Many professional societies have dozens of volunteer committees, councils, divisions, boards, and task forces, each of which oversees a particular area and many of which recommend policies to the board. The important committees are assigned staff members who arrange for meetings, help to prepare agendas, take minutes, and follow up on decisions. While the staff may have a major hand in directing committee work, they typically do not run the committees or use them for support and advice in the way that staff with trade associations do.

To be an elected leader of a professional society is in most cases a mark of distinction. In addition to potential academic or professional advancement, elected leadership also affords significant exposure to the members and, in many cases, to the larger society beyond the membership. The average chief elected officer spends about one-third of his or her time on association business, but many spend 50 percent or more time on activities such as meetings, consulting with the CSE, traveling, and speaking to local member groups. In the American Society of Civil Engineers, a chief elected officer sometimes takes a year's leave of absence from employment to serve the association full-time.

Professional societies embody a number of characteristics relevant to their leadership mode, which are listed next.

- Their boards tend to be larger than those of other associations, probably to accommodate regional and subdisciplinary representatives. The average board size among the professional societies surveyed is 22 members, almost one-third larger than the boards of trade associations with individual members. Turnover among board members is higher than in other types of associations, with the average board member serving four years, almost a year less than board members of trade associations.

- Professional societies tend to employ executive committees to oversee the administration of the association more often (82 percent) than trade associations (76 percent). This may be because their boards are larger and therefore less able to exercise the amount of control desired over the affairs of the society.

- Professional societies experience contested elections for the chief elected officer in 58 percent of the cases, compared with 29 percent of elections in trade associations. Frequency of competitive elections generally correlates with a volunteer-driven leadership mode.

- The CSE is accountable to the chief elected officer rather than to the board or executive committee more often in professional societies (32 percent) than in trade associations (25 percent). Such accountability correlates to some extent with a volunteer-driven association.

- The publications of professional societies are judged by their CSEs to be more volunteer-driven than those of either type of trade association: 6.52 versus 8.00 on a nine-point scale.

- The average tenure of senior staff is shorter than that of their trade association counterparts. Senior staff serve an average of 6.88 years in professional societies and 8.00 years in trade associations. A shorter length of service for senior staff correlates with a volunteer-driven association.

- Counterpart volunteer committees are no more common in professional societies than in trade associations, nor are the committees of professional associations judged to be significantly more directive of staff than in other associations.

- Dues account for a lower percentage of total income in professional societies than in other associations. Professional societies report an average of 42.6 percent of income from dues, compared with 52 percent in trade associations. Professional societies often find it more difficult to raise dues than trade associations, because the money comes from individuals and because members may gain few direct benefits other than meetings, which usually cost extra, and the magazine. Many professional societies have delegate assemblies empowered to approve or reject proposed dues increases, with the consequence that dues increases are difficult to pass and the societies are forced to rely more heavily on nondues income to pay for services.

- Over the past ten years, professional societies have shifted to a staff-driven mode more dramatically than trade associations (table 5).

Table 5

Comparative Prevalence of Leadership Modes, 1978 and 1988

Type of Association	Volunteer-Driven		Balanced		Staff-Driven	
	1978	1988	1978	1988	1978	1988
Professional societies	59%	15%	23%	44%	18%	41%
Trade associations						
corporate members	29	7	27	33	44	60
individual members	33	18	30	38	37	44

Philanthropic Health and Social Welfare or Social Service Associations

As mentioned previously, philanthropic associations focus on a cause, a social problem, or an area of interest or concern. Recruited primarily for their financial support, members often do not vote or volunteer their time or expertise. These organizations are, however, increasing their political activity and are looking to large memberships to add to their political clout.

The members of a philanthropic association have a personal or philosophical affinity for the organization. Rarely does membership in a philanthropic association directly advance the member's personal financial situation. (An exception is some medical specialties affiliated with voluntary health organizations, where affiliation may result in research grants, academic perquisites, or professional or community recognition.)

Volunteer leaders are frequently chosen from among those who contribute financially, give their time, or benefit the association through connections. Volunteers may serve on the board or as elected officers indefinitely; most organizations, however, rotate officers and board members to allow for new blood.

Health and social service or social welfare philanthropic associations are more staff-driven than volunteer-driven; 40 percent of the health associations and 42 percent of the social welfare or social service associations are primarily staff-driven. Another 54 percent of both kinds of associations function with a balanced influence between staff and volunteers. Only 6 percent of the health associations and 4 percent of the social welfare or social service associations report being volunteer-driven.

As in most associations, the volunteer leaders in philanthropic groups approve policy decisions and in that sense help direct the organization. In many cases, volunteers do much of the work of the organization, particularly in fund-raising and organizing special events. Staff, however, take the basic initiatives for new programs and activities and provide essential ongoing administrative and programmatic support.

Some major differences among philanthropic health and social welfare or social service associations affect the extent of a staff- or volunteer-driven mode. The revenue profile for philanthropic social welfare or social service associations is quite

Table 6

Sources of Revenue for Philanthropic Associations

Source of Revenue	Philanthropic Health Associations	Philanthropic Social Welfare, Social Service Associations
Contributions	74.5%	32.2%
Dues	3.8	16.3
The United Way	3.9	8.2
Publications and advertising	2.5	2.7
Education programs	2.5	2.3
Meetings	1.7	2.3
Investments	5.1	5.0
Insurance programs	—	1.3
Government	1.7	5.2
Services	0.6	7.3
Other (contracts, special events, grants, merchandise sales, and so forth)	3.7	17.2
Total	100.0	100.0

different from philanthropic health associations (table 6). Social service or social welfare associations are more member oriented, depend more on United Way funding, provide more services for a fee, and look more to the federal and state governments for grants and contracts than philanthropic health associations. The latter depend more on public contributions and large donations. In both cases, the sources of revenue require that staff actively direct the affairs of the association, with technical skills and continuity of relationships that only paid staff can deliver.

The characteristics of philanthropic health associations, listed next, distinguish them from philanthropic social welfare or social service associations.

• Board members of health associations serve an average of 6.12 years, a year longer than board members of social welfare or social service associations, who serve an average of 5.09 years. Longer board service correlates with a staff-driven leadership mode.

• The chief elected officers of philanthropic health associations spend less time, on average, on association business (15 percent) than the chief elected officers of philanthropic social welfare or social service associations (22.6 percent). Lower percentages of time correlate with a staff-driven leadership mode.

• Volunteer committees are more influential in setting the basic tone and direction in health organizations than in social welfare or social service associations.

• Individual board members and volunteer committees are more involved in the day-to-day work of philanthropic health associations than in social welfare or social service associations.

• Philanthropic health associations more often have counterpart volunteer committees to staff departments than social welfare or social service associations. Seventy percent of the health associations report that most or all staff departments have volunteer committees, compared with 46 percent of social welfare or social service associations. More health associations than social welfare or social service organizations report that volunteer committees are advisory to staff rather than directive.

Philanthropic social welfare or social service associations include United Way organizations, the Girl Scouts, American Red Cross, Family Service associations, consumer groups, Foster Parents plans, YMCA, and similar organizations. There are thousands of these organizations at the international, national, regional, state, and local levels; all are organized with volunteer governance and committees and a relatively small paid staff, if any.

Some of the salient, distinguishing characteristics of philanthropic social welfare or social service associations are enumerated next.

• Growth of these associations over the past decade has outpaced that of health associations. The full-time staffs have grown from an average of 36.7 individuals in 1978 to 50.7 in 1988, an increase of 38 percent. During the same period, the staffs of health associations grew from an average of 24.3 to 29.4 individuals, an increase of 21 percent.

- The length of service of the CSE and other senior staff is almost a year longer in these associations than in health associations, 7.9 versus 7.0 years. Longer tenure generally correlates with a staff-driven organization.

- Social welfare or social service associations designate their chief staff executive as CEO more often (52 percent) than their health association counterparts (33 percent). The CEO designation tends to indicate a staff-driven association.

- The CSE in a social welfare or social service association is a voting member of the board more often (20 percent of the cases) than in philanthropic health associations (3 percent).

- In these associations, the most influential body in setting the basic tone and direction is the board, whereas in philanthropic health associations, it is more often the executive committee and senior staff.

- Social welfare or social service associations do strategic planning more often (62 percent) than health associations (48 percent). They reported that strategic planning has increased the staff influence in association affairs.

- The CSEs of these associations act more unilaterally in personnel and budget areas than their counterparts in philanthropic health associations. Sixty-three percent of the CSEs of social welfare or social service associations reported that they hire, fire, and promote staff without the approval of volunteer leaders, compared with 44 percent of those of health associations, who more often first seek leaders' approval. In the budget area, the CSEs of social welfare or social service associations have slightly more latitude in exceeding budget and shifting expenditures among line items than the CSEs of health associations.

Despite these differences, the leadership modes of philanthropic health and social welfare or social service associations are similar. On the nine-point scale (0 equaling totally volunteer-driven, 9 equaling totally staff-driven), health associations averaged 5.44 and social welfare or social service associations, 5.73.

Chapter 6

The Role of Committees

Volunteer committees deserve special comment. Their role and relation to staff play an important part in determining whether an association is staff- or volunteer-driven. The temptation is to assign an association's leadership mode based on the board and the chief elected officer and their relationships to the chief staff executive (CSE), but volunteer committees merit equal consideration.

Some volunteer committees center around the key functional activities of the association, such as publications, education, conventions, government affairs, membership, fund-raising, and chapter services. Others are tied to various segments of the membership, such as industry or geographic subgroups or, in the case of a professional society, specialty areas. Still other committees focus on issues or subjects, such as product standards or environmental concerns. In addition, there may be various ad hoc committees, such as strategic planning or governance task forces, and committees of the board, such as executive, finance, personnel, bylaws, and nominations. Associations may have dozens or even hundreds of committees and subcommittees absorbing the energies of thousands of volunteers.

Volunteer-driven associations usually have powerful volunteer committees (see chapter 4). Among trade and professional associations that have counterpart volunteer committees, almost 40 percent of the volunteer-driven organizations reported that the committees, staffed by senior staff members, direct the activities of the departments they oversee. For staff-driven associations, the figure is 20 percent. In philanthropic associations, 65 percent of the volunteer-driven organizations reported that committees direct staff activities, compared with 16 percent of staff-driven associations. The differences are very significant and play an important role in determining whether an association is volunteer- or staff-driven.

Staff-driven associations have fewer counterpart committees, and these tend to be advisory to, rather than directive of, the work of the staff. Advisory committees serve to generate ideas for the staff or provide particular kinds of expertise that the staff need but may not have, such as in finance, data processing, or industry topics.

Through committees, volunteers can exercise a powerful influence in an association. Committees involve the largest body of volunteers, and their influence is felt throughout the association. Committees do much of the work of associations. Volunteer time, energy, and experience supplement staff time, energy, and expertise. Indeed, much of the art of running a successful association consists of obtaining enough time and energy from enough volunteers in committees so that useful work is accomplished.

Most significant volunteer committees are supported by staff members. In some cases, staff support is logistical, such as scheduling and arranging for meeting space. More extensive support entails preparing meeting minutes, working with committee chairs to prepare agendas, and following up meetings by gathering information, researching, and telephoning.

In Volunteer-Driven Associations

More volunteer-driven associations have counterpart committees that parallel staff departments than staff-driven associations: 45 percent of volunteer-driven trade and professional associations and 70 percent of volunteer-driven philanthropic associations, compared with 32 percent of staff-driven trade and professional associations and 51 percent of staff-driven philanthropic associations.

Decisions of counterpart committees affect departmental budgets, priorities, programs, and the way staff spend their time. In extreme cases, the committee and staff department act like an autonomous mini-association.

Powerful committees can be a very constructive force in the association, and they impart to the participating volunteers a sense of making an impact on the direction and functioning of the organization. If they are accountable to the board, strong committees can act to magnify its power and influence over the activities of the association. However, when volunteer committees get too strong, they can undercut and disrupt established patterns of accountability.

In one association, a volunteer committee had its own source of income from special conferences. Technically part of the association's overall budget, the income was earmarked for this committee's use. When the committee felt that too few staff members were assigned to it, it hired additional staff on a contract basis, paid from its "own" funds. The committee also pressed for salary increases for the principal staffer serving it; these increases exceeded those granted to other staff members, and the committee used its independent income and a threat to split off from the association as wedges to circumvent the regular staff salary schedule. Neither the board nor the CSE was able to assert authority over the committee. The results were grumbling from other volunteers, lowered staff morale, and a reduction in the board's ability to govern the association.

Handling committee relationships can complicate the CSE's life when the committee chair also sits on the board. The board member/committee chair can develop a close relationship with the subordinate staff member who serves the committee, particularly if the chair relies heavily on the staffer for information or meeting preparation. In some cases, the staffer enlists the board member/committee chair as an advocate in matters such as departmental budgets, programs, meetings, and the like. This relationship can put the CSE in a difficult spot. If the CSE attempts to limit the staff member's budget, transfer the staff member's duties, or otherwise take action that the staff member believes is not in his or her best interests or in those of the department or committee, the staff member may be able to exert pressure through the committee chair/board member that effectively limits the CSE's authority. In effect, the staff member builds an independent power base and becomes insulated from the CSE's actions and decisions.

In these cases, the staff members may genuinely believe that they are acting in the best interests of their associations. They may view their primary accountability as being to the committee chair and their primary job as serving that committee. They may also be aware that having an independent base of support on the board represents protection of a sort and the possibility for an increased budget allocation. In the long run, however, such an arrangement hurts the association: It weakens the chain of accountability and undercuts the CSE's ability to manage affairs.

In the best cases, an arrangement is tacitly or explicitly worked out that makes the staff person primarily accountable to the CSE and secondarily accountable to the committee chair. The key people involved—the staff person serving the committee, the committee chair, the CSE, and the chief elected officer—agree to this arrangement and abide by it. Thus, the CSE can manage staff resources to serve the needs of all committees and provide for a consistent and appropriate level of support to the entire committee structure without the fear that an executive decision will hurt his or her relationship with the board.

In order for this arrangement to work, however, committee chairs, board members, and officers must know and abide by the rules. These rules, in turn, must be reinforced by the chief elected officer, who does not permit a board member to lobby for the budget, programs, or particular interests of a staff member over the CSE's objections. The CSE must also reinforce the arrangement by clarifying for staff members who serve committees the association's overall priorities, expectations of the committees, and the absolute requirement that staff members communicate committee activities.

As mentioned, finances frequently pose a special problem. Separate, independent sources of income that "belong" to the committee or to the staff department that the committee oversees can cause real management problems. The less control that the board and CSE exercise, the greater potential for problems, including having the committee split off to form another association and taking some of the members with it. The usual preventive measure is to consider all revenue generated by components of the association as the association's revenue and to put the monies into the general funds. Budgets for committees, departments, divisions, and other components are determined separately and approved by the board, without reference to the revenue they generate. Successful associations find it important for all volunteers and staff in leadership positions to play by these rules and not insist that certain groups in the association have special status because of the funds they bring in.

In volunteer-driven associations, the staff member serving the committee often takes a more passive role than in staff-driven associations. In preparing for committee meetings, staff members in volunteer-driven associations usually consult with the committee chair to prepare the agenda, but the chair determines the agenda items and specifies desired outcomes.

During meetings, the staff member may take notes for minute preparation, handle logistics, report on the activities of the department, and serve as a technical resource. Meeting minutes are extensive and are distributed soon after the meeting. Committee members and staff treat the minutes as directives for follow-up or to take to the board for approval.

In a volunteer-driven association, the actions of committees can make a significant impact on the department. An education committee, for example, may determine program content, mode of delivery (for example, seminars, short or extended courses, and programs to be held in conjunction with association-wide meetings), the instructors and their fees, sites, promotional materials, program fees, and other operational matters. As another example, a publications committee may decide the ratio of advertising to editorial content, advertising guidelines, which articles to accept or reject, and subscription costs, among other matters.

Committee chairs in volunteer-driven associations frequently are highly influential, particularly if the committee's area is technical and not well understood by the board. Standards activities are a good case in point. Boards are generally reluctant to meddle in the standards activities of their associations and prefer to leave decisions to appropriate committees and staff. The chair of a standards committee, by determining what the committee takes up and how decisions are made, can thus effectively direct the activities of the association.

Sometimes, committee influence can be excessive and, if combined with a lack of accountability, can do real damage. In one trade association, the education committee chair, who was also an instructor, determined the association's educational policy, including the fees paid to instructors and the choice of suppliers of educational materials. As a committee chair, he also served on the board. Because the board operated under the implicit agreement that members would not infringe on one another's areas and because the association was heavily volunteer-driven, there was little accountability for the education function. Over time, instructors' fees became exorbitant and the pool of instructors essentially a closed shop, with the result that the education program failed to reach its potential. The situation was rectified only by the retirement of the committee chair and his replacement by an individual who was not an instructor.

In Staff-Driven Associations

In staff-driven associations, committees tend to be advisory. Eighty percent of the respondents in staff-driven trade and professional associations and 84 percent in staff-driven philanthropic associations said that committees mainly advised, rather than directed, the staff.

In staff-driven associations, staff members typically take an active or controlling role in committee meetings, summarizing and commenting on discussions and indicating ideas that merit further action. The staff liaison and the chair frequently collaborate on the content and form of reports to the board, without the direct counsel of the committee itself. The staffer also prepares the agenda in consultation with the chair and takes the lead in proposing agenda items and indicating desired outcomes. As in volunteer-driven associations, the staffer prepares the minutes. Minutes may be included in the advance materials to the next meeting but are often not used again because few decisions, if any, need follow-up.

In the extreme, committees in staff-driven associations can become so de-energized that they cease to function, even to advise the appropriate staff department. Attendance drops, meetings become infrequent, and gradually the committee fades from existence.

Boards can react in similar fashion, particularly if they function simply to ratify the CSE's actions and to receive staff reports. In such instances, the volunteer leaders may perceive that the board needs to act in order to restore any vitality. There may, thus, be attempts to revitalize the board by seeking its decisions. Often, these efforts cannot be sustained, and the board falls back to its old mode of functioning until there is a staff shake-up.

Committees in staff-driven associations may discuss ideas, make suggestions to staff, and, on occasion, make recommendations to the board for action. However, they typically do not direct staff work or set priorities. The committee may be asked to brainstorm, but staff are freer than in volunteer-driven associations to select from among the suggestions offered and less compelled to report on actions taken.

Chapter 7

Benefits and Drawbacks of the Leadership Modes

T his chapter enumerates and explores the positive and negative aspects associated with each leadership mode, based on the responses of the chief staff executives (CSEs) surveyed.

The Volunteer-Driven Mode

Benefits

In trade and professional associations, the most frequently mentioned benefit (53 percent) of the volunteer-driven leadership mode is that it fosters member interest, involvement, and pride in the association. Trade associations executives cited this benefit as much more important than other benefits, whereas professional society executives ranked it marginally more important than other benefits, such as access to new ideas and efficiency.

Among philanthropic associations, the most important benefit deriving from the volunteer-driven mode is volunteer dedication, participation, and support, including financial support. Of the CSEs who mentioned the benefits of a volunteer-driven association, 65 percent cited this as most important.

The ability to obtain a variety of expertise from volunteers was mentioned next most frequently (34 percent) in philanthropic associations. Volunteers skilled in planning, accounting, the law, legislative affairs, general management, and special event management are particularly valued in philanthropic associations whose staff do not possess those skills in depth.

The second most important benefit to trade and professional societies (21 percent) is that a volunteer-driven association occupies a better position to know the needs of the members and to mount programs to meet those needs. Because of volunteer involvement in the direction of the association, CSEs felt that they could better identify needs, initiate programs to respond to those needs, and give the programs sufficient priority to enable implementation.

In philanthropic associations, 21 percent cited community involvement and awareness as a benefit of a volunteer-driven association. This benefit was particularly important among social welfare or social service associations. In a way, this benefit is analogous to the benefit of meeting member needs cited among trade and professional associations. Volunteer involvement gives the association perspective and helps to keep the staff focused.

For trade and professional associations, the next most frequently mentioned benefit is access to new ideas and fresh perspectives (16 percent). Again, the CSEs' concerns are a myopic view of the association and the antidote is volunteer involvement.

A few respondents stated that a volunteer-driven association can operate at lower costs than a staff-driven organization, because volunteer time is free. To some extent, this is true, particularly in trade associations where staff from member companies help to carry some of the workload and in philanthropic associations where volunteers are used extensively in fundraising. If members pay their own travel expenses, the savings can be substantial. In standards-making associations, the volunteers' contributions can markedly augment net revenues. Balancing this, however, are the staff costs of supporting volunteers and expenses associated with meetings and communications.

Other benefits cited among trade and professional associations included greater accountability and improved industry image because of volunteer involvement in directing the association.

Sample Responses

The sample survey responses from CSEs that follow illustrate the benefits of a volunteer-driven association.

- "Volunteers are interested in the association and therefore perform their jobs well."

- "More involvement, which develops more ownership, which results in more broad-based advocacy of the association's goals, activities, and actions."

- "More enlightened and enthusiastic membership."

- "More loyal membership."

- "New ideas, fresh perspectives."

- "Availability of a large pool of interested and capable leaders."

- "Improved industry image because of volunteer involvement."

- "Stronger lobbying program because the members provide technical substance about the industry that staff can't provide."

- "Greater awareness of industry problems."

- "Greater acceptance of the reality of industry conditions."

- "Members willing to make significant commitments of time to help other members."

- "Use of volunteers saves money."

- "Better local implementation of programs that are both national and local in scope."

- "More sensitivity to and sharper focus on activities that benefit the members."

- "An understanding that the association belongs to the members."

- "A great feeling of brotherhood and friendship. Many recruits and individuals to call upon."

- "More responsive to the needs of the membership; members take a more responsible role in working to meet those needs."

- "Talented, enthusiastic resources at low cost to the organization."
- "Broad spectrum of people to tap for fund-raising and service projects."
- "The potential for growth and development is far greater."
- "Local visibility and representation."

Drawbacks

The most frequently cited drawback of a volunteer-driven association is the length of time required to make decisions and reach consensus on issues requiring action; 26 percent of the trade and professional associations and 62 percent of the philanthropic associations indicated this. The problem concerns the infrequent meetings of boards and committees, which force a delay on decisions requiring volunteer action. Another part of the problem involves the time needed to gain the concurrence of several people in decision making, as opposed to one person or a few people who can simply decide. When the board of a volunteer-driven association is not in session, for example, the CSE may need to convince several people by telephone about the need for a decision. This can often be a frustrating and time-consuming endeavor. Additionally, volunteer committees may need to review proposals and decisions before the board is willing to act, and committee chairs may not assign these the same degree of urgency as the CSE.

The second most frequently mentioned drawback in trade and professional associations (20 percent) concerns a lack of organization and control. Volunteer-driven associations are untidy. Several or many people are frequently involved in decisions. There may be overlapping jurisdictions among committees. It is sometimes unclear, in advance, whether a move is major or trivial. There are many different sensitivities to acknowledge and attend to.

The third most frequent drawback for trade and professional associations involves problems in getting the volunteers to complete work (17 percent). Volunteers often have other higher priorities than the work of the association. Business, professional, and personal commitments can and do take precedence over association work. Other than commenting on performance, complaining to the chief elected officer, or engineering a volunteer's removal from a position, a CSE or an association officer has few ways to penalize a failure to meet commitments.

Unprofessional and generally low-quality volunteer work was frequently mentioned as a problem in trade and professional associations (14 percent). Volunteers may have neither the time nor the need to deliver to the association the sort of quality work demanded in their businesses or professions. Moreover, volunteers may head up areas they know little about and may not avail themselves of expertise among the staff or outside resources. An example is an education program where volunteers developed the course material without consulting staff education professionals.

Inconsistency is a problem for several trade and professional respondents. Volunteer leaders and committee chairs turn over. If the association has no strategic plan to guide it or if an existing plan is given only lip service, the priorities of the association can and do change to reflect the individual desires of the current volunteer leaders. Initiatives and programs that span more than one year may derail and languish because their original volunteer supporters are no longer involved. This can wreak havoc with the staff, who cannot plan for the long term, and can waste resources on activities that have only marginal long-term value.

Other mentioned drawbacks include tension between volunteers and staff, excessive staff time needed to train and support volunteers, volunteers who stay too long as committee chairs, and volunteers' resistance to change.

Sample Responses

The sample survey responses that follow further illustrate the drawbacks of volunteer-driven associations.

- "Committee processes take time."

- "Mutual sharing of organization's goals by staff and volunteers takes training and development, which complicates things."

- "Planning goes out the window. We change directions too fast."
- "Unable to keep up with rapid growth."
- "Unprofessional image."
- "Efficiency can suffer because of lack of follow-through."
- "Impossible to penalize late or insufficient work on the part of volunteers."
- "Major tasks are sometimes given to committees that don't do the work."
- "Harder to get agreement on direction for the organization."
- "Constant turnover of people. Difficulty in follow-through, especially on ideas requiring more than a year to pay off."
- "Inconsistency, uneven performance, variability from year to year."
- "Initiating programs is more time-consuming."
- "Longer decision-making process; takes longer to get things done."
- "Volunteers don't have responsibility for resources, yet can make decisions."
- "Increased staff load with letter writing and phone time; greater need to organize and communicate relevant information to the members."
- "Sometimes it's difficult to rein in wild horses."
- "Volunteer leaders are on the scene for a short time, do their damage, and then run off to mess things up somewhere else."
- "Nitpicking."
- "Higher stress level in the staff."
- "Volunteers sometimes see staff as 'servants.' "
- "Volunteers can too easily get too deeply involved in the management of the association."
- "Amateurism."

- "Repetition of the errors of the past."
- "Things take longer because we get bogged down in process."
- "Sometimes our volunteer leadership does not have sufficient data to make good decisions."
- "Lack of professional attitudes on the part of volunteers."
- "Personality conflicts interfere with the well-being of the organization."
- "Never trust your bookkeeping or tax matters to a volunteer, no matter how well-intentioned that volunteer may be!"

The Staff-Driven Mode

Benefits

The principal benefit of a staff-driven association is its operating efficiency, as indicated by 34 percent of the trade and professional associations and 23 percent of the philanthropic associations. Staff-driven management enables work to be accomplished more quickly and easily than volunteer-driven management. Staff members assigned tasks can be held accountable. Decisions can be made quickly and with a minimum of consultation. New programs can be implemented with little concurrence from others.

The next most frequently mentioned benefit is consistency, cited by 28 percent of the trade and professional associations and 29 percent of the philanthropic associations. Volunteers come and go; staff stay around. Programs and projects with a life longer than a year can be mounted with the expectation that the responsible staffer will be there for the duration. Unlike a volunteer-driven association, a staff-driven association does not have to suffer from work of inconsistent quality.

Related to consistency is another benefit: Real expertise can be brought to bear on a problem or assignment. A staff-driven association has more latitude in deciding who is best qualified to handle a project, either a staff member or an outside resource.

In a volunteer-driven association, there is pressure to assign the problem to the committee with jurisdiction over the area, regardless of the members' expertise. By applying expertise, a job can be done more professionally.

A fourth benefit is the responsiveness of staff members. When staff members are asked to do a job by the CSE, they can be expected to respond affirmatively and to deliver. In a volunteer-driven association, the response to a request can be muted and equivocal. Volunteers are frequently reluctant to assume work, and when they do, it may not meet the requirements of the person making the request.

Other benefits include objectivity, broader perspective on situations, better motivation by workers, and more control by management.

Sample Responses

Sample responses about the benefits of the staff-driven leadership mode are enumerated next.

- "Able to react more quickly to situations."

- "Things get done."

- "Freedom to pursue areas the staff believe are important."

- "More flexibility."

- "Time is saved by being able to go ahead with programs without waiting for approval from volunteers. New programs get on line faster."

- "Continuity and stability."

- "Better control and accountability."

- "The association can operate more efficiently because the number of meetings is reduced."

- "Lower cost for volunteer travel means more money available for salaries and equipment."

- "Thoroughness."

- "Association jobs done by people who have a primary, not a secondary, interest in the association."

- "More professional expertise brought to bear on a situation. Staff able to develop a level of expertise higher than that of the membership."

- "Staff are more objective and serve the needs of the entire membership without prejudice."

- "Don't have to spend time and energy securing volunteers."

- "Better control of finances."

- "Same people dealing with legislators promotes better working relationships and more consistent action."

- "Able to attract and hold more qualified staff."

- "Members more open with comments and suggestions without fear of being assigned to volunteer work."

- "Large dues payers are assured of a return on their investment."

- "Staff are not weighted down with committee work."

- "We must look at nonprofit organizations as a business operation. What business could operate efficiently with part-time volunteers?"

Drawbacks

The chief drawback of a staff-driven association, according to the respondents, is a lack of member interest in association affairs. That translates into a lack of volunteer involvement in activities and a lack of commitment to organizational goals. Twenty percent of the respondents indicated this disadvantage. If the staff run things, members can become apathetic and lose much of their interest in the association. The members may view the association not as theirs but as a place that provides certain services, such as insurance, a magazine, and education programs. As one respondent said, "The association takes on the characteristics of a library, with the members as patrons. How long has it been since you were passionately interested in your public library?"

A lack of volunteer direction can mean difficulties in getting people to serve on committees, to run for office, and to serve on the board. There may be a sense that these activities are meaningless except, perhaps, to advance one's career or industry position. When volunteers choose not to get involved, the association is deprived of their expertise in the industry or profession. This can be a serious deficit and can lead the association into taking positions or mounting programs that members do not support.

A third and related problem is the potential for misunderstanding and miscommunication between the members and the staff. The staff can lose touch with the members and their needs. Communications thin out. The staff may view the members as sources of income and nothing more. The members may view the staff as the "enemy" or wonder what staff are doing with their money.

Staff in a staff-driven association are open to significantly more criticism than in a volunteer-driven association. Staff members make and are accountable for decisions affecting the members. It is not possible to respond to criticism by saying, "Your fellow members made the decision, so take it up with them." A them-versus-us climate can develop. Staff members may feel the need to adopt a protective posture, which exacerbates the problem.

Several respondents said that a staff-driven mode makes for a higher-cost association. Work that could be accomplished free of charge by volunteers is performed for pay by staff. The reverse argument is that volunteer work is not free, often costing expenses and staff time.

Sample Responses

The sample responses that follow illuminate the drawbacks of a staff-driven association.

- "Staff sometimes feel out on a limb. Your scalp is on the line."
- "Staff are overworked; demands for performance often exceed the staff time available."
- "Staff must assume more responsibility for mistakes."

- "Staff not as close to member needs as volunteers are; potential trap of becoming insulated from changing member needs; lack of sensitivity to issues; ivory tower syndrome."

- "General lack of member involvement."

- "Members may not be supportive when things get tough."

- "Goals may not be achieved if budget is not large enough to provide for staff to do the job."

- "As staff increase, volunteers perceive that their contributions are no longer critical, and therefore slack off. Member apathy becomes a problem when staff do a good job."

- "Staff sometimes feel like they are beating a dead horse."

- "Members less likely to solicit new members."

- "Easier to drop membership if not involved at one time or another."

- "Harder to find and build volunteer leaders to serve on the board and in other capacities."

- "Need to work to keep charges of favoritism to a minimum (small versus large, rural versus urban)."

- "Individual members may disagree with a decision and challenge the staff."

- "Members don't feel part of the association."

- "Must constantly watch for the them-versus-us feeling."

- "Less volunteer investment in outcomes."

- "Less input of ideas."

- "Requires more selling because members do not always see the efforts of the staff."

- "Perspective of the organization is narrowed by too much staff direction."

- "An ineffective staff can destroy the organization."

- "Diminished community support because of lack of involvement of community persons at the grass-roots level."

Which Mode Is Better?

Given the benefits and drawbacks of volunteer-driven and staff-driven associations, is one better than the other? The answer is, of course, it depends. It depends on the purpose of the association and its needs to grow and develop.

An association that requires substantive member feedback about their needs and conditions in the industry or profession, as well as members' time and energy to accomplish its work, will do better as a volunteer-driven organization. An association that has a core set of activities which require consistent, long-term, professional management will do better as a staff-driven organization. This is particularly true if the association is in competition with for-profit entities in such areas as publications, meetings, and education.

In many ways, the adoption of one leadership mode over the other is a trade-off. The CSE of a volunteer-driven association has to manage a certain amount of sloppy performance and lack of control in order to gain the benefits and strengths of member involvement and participation. The CSE of a staff-driven association has to live with a certain amount of isolation, criticism, and lack of understanding from members about the staff in order to gain the benefits of greater efficiency and consistency.

Can a CSE have it both ways? The answer is, yes, to an extent. Having it both ways is explored in the next chapter.

Chapter 8

A Balanced Mode: The Third Alternative

O f the 232 trade and professional associations surveyed, 37 percent characterized themselves as being both volunteer-driven and staff-driven, that is, as functioning with a balanced leadership mode. Of the 188 philanthropic associations, 49 percent rated their leadership mode as balanced. These respondents ranked their organizations as approximately midway between the volunteer- and staff-driven extremes and felt that initiatives and direction from both sources were important.

Sample Responses

Presented next are sample descriptions from chief staff executives (CSEs) of associations with a balanced mode. A common element in these associations is for volunteers to contribute their knowledge and staff to manage internal affairs that result from that knowledge. The CSEs agree that the roles of volunteers and staff must be delineated specifically so that they can work together.

- "Staff work with the board and committees to create new projects and service ongoing activities."

- "The board takes the lead in setting policy, but staff do the spadework. On programs, staff and key volunteers have leadership roles and responsibilities. It is very important not to have volunteers do nitty-gritty or focus on internal management issues, but to get them to focus and use their time on providing field experience that the staff cannot provide.''

- ''A balance with adequate staff authority; real volunteer interest is ideal but extremely difficult to maintain.''

- ''In our profession, constant changes in the state of the art and regulatory requirements require a great deal of technical input in the operation of the organization. It would be cost prohibitive to try to provide all the necessary expertise on staff. On the other hand, the management and administration of the organization is best handled by staff with board oversight.''

- ''Balance of both volunteer- and staff-driven, together with clearly defined roles and responsibilities, are essential for long-term success.''

- ''The chief staff executive must achieve a balance between the two. The association will suffer if either staff or volunteers have too much power.''

- ''This issue [staff-driven versus volunteer-driven] is largely determined by the members' environment and the competency of the chief staff executive. The best associations achieve a balance, a dynamic tension, between staff and volunteers.''

- ''In professional/technical societies, the members drive when technical expertise or product content is the issue but leave business aspects to staff.''

- ''I believe that volunteers should always be the ones who decide on association programs and services, with staff input. The role of staff in this process is to encourage volunteers to keep their focus on the needs of the field and deal on the policy/program level.''

- ''There must be a good balance so that volunteers feel a part of the association. There must be a feeling of involvement and ownership.''

- ''A trade association should have good staff to make the association perform well, and they should be good enough to merit the confidence of the industry. Members should set policy, priorities, and provide input and support."

- "In a smaller scientific/engineering society such as ours, you need a good mix. Usually, volunteers let the chief staff executive run the office, manage the budget (which is totally staff prepared), and sell publications and advertising. Staff let the members write papers, plan technical meeting programs, and so forth."

- "A good balance is necessary, and we still need a bit more volunteer participation. I am a strong advocate of broad membership participation with strong staff direction."

- "I have witnessed a large swing toward more hands-on volunteer participation in the last 15 years, largely because volunteer leadership is spending more time and is better prepared to lead."

- "I subscribe to a partner or shared responsibility philosophy. There are occasions when initiative should come from volunteers and times when initiatives should emanate from staff."

- "We're staff-driven regarding administrative management and volunteer-driven with respect to overall policy. Seems a good balance at present with little overlap or infringement. Nevertheless, even policy development relies on staff help and input, and management depends on volunteer support."

- "Our organization has reached a balance, with the board determining policy, planning, and evaluation and the staff accountable for operations. Clear distinction between policy and operations."

Characteristics

The balanced mode may be found all along the spectrum, among national, state, and local groups; professional, trade, and philanthropic associations; and large, medium, and small organizations. Associations with a balanced mode share many characteristics, described next.

Growth

The growth among trade and professional associations with a balanced mode is impressive, outdistancing groups with the other two leadership modes on the staff and income measures (table 7).

Among philanthropic associations, the picture looks different (table 8). Using staff and income as measures, the growth among philanthropic associations with a balanced mode has been slower than in either staff- or volunteer-driven groups.

Table 7

Comparisons of Growth Among the Three Leadership Modes in Trade and Professional Associations, 1978 to 1988

Leadership Mode	Growth from 1978 to 1988		
	Membership	Staff	Income
Staff-driven	45%	32%	91%
Volunteer-driven	10	38	23
Balanced	34	53	110

Table 8

Comparisons of Growth Among the Three Leadership Modes in Philanthropic Associations, 1978 to 1988

Leadership Mode	Growth from 1978 to 1988	
	Staff	Income
Staff-driven	35%	77%
Volunteer-driven	34	72
Balanced	29	37

Efficiency

As one measure of efficiency, the changes in the ratio of members to staff over a decade were examined. Trade and professional associations with a balanced mode had the best record for efficiency, increasing the member-to-staff ratio by 10.3 percent over the period (table 9).

Table 9

Comparisons of Member-to-Staff Ratios in Trade and Professional Associations, 1978 to 1988

	Members:Staff		Percentage Change
Leadership Mode	1978	1988	1978 to 1988
Staff-driven*	89.5:1	98.2:1	9.7 %
Volunteer-driven*	586.4:1	340.6:1	(41.9)
Balanced	257.2:1	283.8:1	10.3

*The ratios for staff-driven associations are lower than those for volunteer-driven associations because trade associations, predominantly staff-driven, generally comprise fewer numbers of members than other types of associations.

Stability

Trade and professional associations with a balanced mode have more stable management than staff- or volunteer-driven associations, evidenced by the length of service of CSEs and senior staff. CSEs have a significantly longer tenure in organizations with a balanced mode than in staff-driven or volunteer-driven associations, and senior staffs have about the same tenure as staff-driven groups (table 10).

In philanthropic associations with a balanced mode, the CSE's length of service is shorter than in either staff- or volunteer-driven associations (table 10), whereas the average tenure of senior staffs falls midway between the other two modes. The implication is that a philanthropic association with a balanced mode offers a CSE no greater assurance of long tenure than a staff- or volunteer-driven organization; indeed, a volunteer-driven organization correlates with longer tenure.

Table 10

Comparisons by Leadership Mode of the Tenure of Chief Staff Executives and Senior Staff (in years)

Leadership Mode	Trade and Professional Associations		Philanthropic Associations	
	Chief Staff Executive	Senior Staff	Chief Staff Executive	Senior Staff
Staff-driven	6.38	7.87	7.36	7.80
Volunteer-driven	5.73	5.88	8.56	7.04
Balanced	7.78	7.56	7.17	7.40

Previous Affiliation of the Chief Staff Executive

The CSEs of associations with a balanced mode tend to be insiders or recruited from other associations more often than the CSEs of staff- or volunteer-driven associations; 53 percent of the CSEs from trade and professional groups reported that they came from the profession or industry and 33 percent were recruited from another association. Only 14 percent said they were not from the industry or profession or another association, compared with 27 percent of the CSEs in volunteer-driven associations and 32 percent in staff-driven associations.

Approximately 25 percent of the CSEs of trade and professional associations with a staff-driven or balanced mode were previously with the association in another permanent staff capacity. For volunteer-driven associations, the figure is 15 percent. The implication is that staff in a balanced or staff-driven association stand a better chance of being promoted to CSE than those in a volunteer-driven association.

Philanthropic associations with a balanced mode also tend to recruit CSEs from inside more often than staff- or volunteer-driven associations. Recruiting is done either from among the existing staff or the volunteers. Fifty-eight percent of these CSEs reported that they held a previous permanent position with the organization, compared with 42 percent in volunteer-driven and 46 percent in staff-driven organizations. Overall, 35 percent of philanthropic groups with a balanced mode recruited their CSEs from the outside, compared with 43 percent of volunteer-driven and 48 percent of staff-driven organizations. The differences suggest that associations with a balanced mode tend to select known entities as their CSEs.

CAE Designation

Slightly more CSEs of trade and professional associations with a balanced mode have earned the Certified Association Executive (CAE) designation (21 percent) than their counterparts in staff- or volunteer-driven organizations (16 percent). In philanthropic associations, few executives have the CAE designation, although from 13 to 15 percent of their CSEs reported working on it.

Counterpart Committees

These associations have counterpart volunteer committees for staff departments more often then either staff- or volunteer-driven organizations. Among groups with a balanced mode nearly 75 percent of the trade and professional associations reported counterpart committees, compared with 60 percent of staff-driven and 68 percent of volunteer-driven associations. Among philanthropic associations, those with a balanced mode reported a slightly greater incidence of counterpart committees.

The committees of trade and professional organizations with a balanced mode more frequently direct rather than advise the staff departments with which they are concerned; 44 percent, compared with 38 percent in volunteer-driven associations, and 20 percent in staff-driven associations.

Among philanthropic associations, more than 70 percent of the associations with a balanced or staff-driven mode reported that volunteer committees are mainly advisory to staff, compared with 35 percent for volunteer-driven associations.

Board Size

Boards among all types of associations with a balanced mode are larger by 10 to 15 percent than those of staff- or volunteer-driven associations. While this difference is minor, it appears consistently enough to invite speculation that associations with a balanced mode pay more attention to including representatives from various constituencies than either of the other types of associations.

Other

For most other characteristics, the data for associations with a balanced mode fall between or equal those for staff- and volunteer-driven associations. These characteristics include titles, terms of office, tenure of board members, incomes of board members and the CSE, gender of the CSE and chief elected officer, educational levels of the CSE and the board members, incidence of contested elections, the percentage of time the chief elected officer spends on association business, accountability and voting status of the CSE, and so forth. (See chapter 4, for a discussion of these factors.)

Managing a Balanced Mode

The Roles of Volunteers and Staff

In an association with a balanced mode, the basic roles of staff and volunteer leaders sort out to enable staff to direct association matters and volunteers to direct member-related, professional, and industry matters. Staff are responsible for the administrative aspects of the association—arranging meetings, developing budgets, supervising educational programs, publishing, managing membership recruitment, developing statistics on the industry or profession, managing government relations activities, and so forth.

In a trade or professional association, the volunteers provide firsthand understanding of the needs of the industry or profession and technical expertise derived from participation in the field. In a philanthropic association, lay volunteers bring to bear their knowledge of potential contributors, of the need for service from people deeply involved in the issue of concern, and of corporate legal, financial, and marketing matters useful to the association.

Overlap among staff and volunteers is common. In some cases, staff members, particularly long-time employees or staff members recruited from the membership, know more about the industry or profession than some of the volunteer leaders and can contribute their knowledge in committee meetings and other forums. Staff cannot, however, have the same understanding that a member can, because staff do not run a business or practice the profession.

Volunteers may know a lot about the administration and management of organizations. Those from businesses may have had long experience in running complex and dynamic firms. In time, they may come to know much about the association as a whole and the operation of particular departments or functions in particular. In one association, the elected president initiated, organized, and ran the association's planning process, including interviewing staff and volunteers and developing planning information. Nevertheless, volunteers cannot have the firsthand feel that staff have for association operations, because they are not involved 100 percent of the time.

One might, then, think of the roles of staff and volunteers this way: Staff have a primary stake in keeping the association going and growing; volunteers have a primary stake in ensuring that the association serves the needs of the members, including influencing the political, social, and economic environment within which the members function. Staff have experience and technical expertise in the administration and operation of the association; volunteers have experience and expertise in the events and climate of their industry or profession and how these translate into member needs.

Thus, the principal distinction in an association with a balanced mode is that staff carry responsibilities for operating the association and maintaining it in good working order, and the volunteers, responsibilities for providing information that keeps programs and activities focused on the needs of the members, as well as for offering technical expertise to carry on activities affecting the industry or the profession, such as formulating positions on public issues. Policies, that is, general rules which govern specific circumstances, while usually board approved, may be initiated by either staff or volunteers and are not the sole prerogative of one group.

From these distinctions, other parts of the picture flow.

- Committees, including counterpart committees to staff departments, that focus on industry or professional problems generally direct staff activities. Counterpart committees in publications, meetings, insurance, fund-raising, and other areas of staff expertise generally advise and do not direct.

- The board focuses on broad issues facing the industry, profession, or area of concern and on general policy that guides activities such as budgets, dues structure, and approval of significant new programs. It steers from detailed administrative questions of staff, minor budget adjustments, and similar issues within staff purview, unless the CSE raises them.

- Volunteers treat staff members as professionals in association management.

- Staff treat volunteers as experts in the industry or profession.

For the CSE an important aspect of developing and maintaining a balance between staff and volunteer influence in the association is clearly to differentiate their roles in order to foster mutual respect between the groups and an appreciation of the differences each brings. The combination can produce synergisms impossible in either a volunteer-driven or a staff-driven association. This differentiation also helps to prevent each from encroaching too far into the territory of the other. It can help to avoid crippling competition over power and to finesse the question of who's the boss.

Accountability

Accountability in which the lines are explicitly delineated, is essential if an association is to function properly. The ideal chain of accountability extends from the staff at all levels to the CSE and from there to the volunteer leaders and members. The CSE is ultimately accountable for staff, and the board (or its surrogate, the executive committee) for the CSE. The board, in turn, is accountable to the members or constituents of the association.

Without strong accountability, associations can flounder. Staff may lose touch with the members, and volunteer leaders may make policies inimical to the best interests of the members. Portions of the staff may function beyond the control of the CSE and the board. When these things happen, the organization may be in serious trouble.

Several years ago, in one large professional association, a department staff director and his volunteer committee chair, on the advice of legal counsel, decided to litigate a suit filed against the organization. The legal counsel judged that the association would prevail and that a precedent would be set for immunizing the association and others like it from future legal action. The sector of the association concerned had been operating independently because it was involved in a technical area beyond the interests of the board and CSE.

The department director and committee chair functioned essentially as a mini-association. The department director was used to making decisions and informing the CSE about them later. The committee chair also served on the board but reported minimal information about the activities of "his" part of the organization, expecting and receiving nearly automatic approvals of his recommendations. In short, the chain of accountability was broken: The department was not accountable to the CSE, and the committee chair was not accountable to the board.

The decision to litigate was not made within the accountability structure, that is, by the board or CSE after careful deliberation of the risks and alternatives. Instead, it was made by a staff member and committee chair because the chain of accountability was weak.

Rather than settle out of court, the association fought the suit, and the case was tried before a jury. The association was found guilty and assessed a fine and punitive damages that nearly wiped out its reserves.

A strong system of accountability with clear lines of authority is necessary because decisions are often made on estimates of members' need, to avoid conflict, or, as in the litigation example cited, as a result of the urgings of particularly powerful individuals. When an association assesses its performance either in a specific area or as a whole, it usually bases its evaluation on several situationally derived criteria (such as whether budget goals were met, objectives were accomplished, or membership growth was satisfactory). Use of these criteria to judge performance and to make decisions about the use of resources requires an explicit system of accountability, because results are measured against previously made commitments.

A fundamental strategy for managing a balanced leadership mode is to build a structure that ensures accountability. Accountability entails more than monitoring. It is essentially a process of ascertaining whether commitments, general and specific, have been carried out. The process requires that one party (such as the govering board) which delegates responsibility to another party (such as the CSE) be able to ask questions and require satisfactory answers. A system is accountable when the parties at each level are able to delegate, obtain commitments, ask the right questions, and know what constitutes a satisfactory answer.

In staff-driven associations, the CSE's accountability to volunteer leaders is relatively weak because the staff initiates and makes many decisions without volunteer input. In volunteer-driven associations, the staff's accountability to the CSE is relatively weak because volunteer committees strongly influence the time and energies of staff. In a well-functioning system of balance, these accountabilities are relatively strong. One of the CSE's principal jobs is to maintain that balance.

One area in flux in associations is the accountability of volunteer committees. According to conventional wisdom, volunteer committes should be accountable to the chief elected officer and the board in the same way that staff are accountable to the CSE and through the CSE to the board. Increasingly, however, boards are holding the CSE partially responsible for the functioning of volunteer committees, as well as for staff. Volunteer committees are viewed, in this context, as vehicles to do the association's work. The reason is twofold. First, boards are looking to CSEs, not the chief elected officers, as the principal agents to carry out their directions. Second, CSEs are responsible for supplying staff to serve the committees. The way staffs function invariably has a major effect on the productivity of volunteer committees. Thus, according to this line of reasoning, CSEs should be held at least partially responsible for how the committees function.

If this trend continues, the CSEs will move into a more centrally accountable position, with the result that associations will become more staff-driven. In fact, this has been happening in associations over the past decade. Partly as a result, the roles of CSEs and chief elected officers have also been shifting.

Relationship Between the Chief Staff Executive and the Chief Elected Officer

The relationship between the CSE and the chief elected officer is collegial in an association with a balanced mode. The board (or executive committee), not the chief elected officer, is the CSE's boss. Together, the CSE and the chief elected officer represent the two most important constituents of the association—the members and the staff. Each represents a valuable and necessary perspective.

The CSE represents continuity, a deep understanding of the workings of the association, its financial realities and possibilities, and staff capabilities and limitations. The chief elected officer can express the members' point of view, has industry or professional experience, personally knows many of the members and volunteer leaders, and serves as the surrogate for the members.

Role of the Chief Staff Executive

The CSE in an association with a balanced mode can legitimately be called the chief operating officer and, as such, marshals the staff to accomplish the work of the association. The CSE coordinates staff activities, assigns staff responsibilities, and delegates the authority needed to carry out those responsibilities.

The CSE is also responsible for supporting the work of volunteer committees by allocating resources and assigning staff to work with committee chairs in setting goals, developing agendas, serving as an information resource during committee meetings, recording the meetings for future reference, and implementing decisions made during the meeting.

As chief operating officer, the CSE carries many of the following responsibilities:

- reports and is accountable to the board on the status of the association's finances, programs, and functions;

- initiates policy recommendations for board approval;

- helps to shape association priorities with volunteer leaders and senior staff;

- directs budget preparation;

- works closely with the chief elected officer and other volunteer leaders in carrying out the goals of the organization and serves as the board's principal agent in this respect;

- takes an active role in formulating the association's strategic plan; serves on the strategic planning committee and provides necessary staff and other resources to facilitate its work;

- hires, fires, promotes, rewards, and disciplines the staff with the advice of the board, when appropriate (usually in connection with senior staff); ensures useful and appropriate personnel policies to guide daily activities;

- provides necessary staff support to officers and volunteer committees;

- represents the association to CSEs of related associations and coalitions;

- along with the chief elected officer, represents the association to the public, government agencies, and the members;

- actively promotes the association at meetings of the members;

- ensures that the needs of all members are met within the limits of the association's finances and the directives of the board.

Role of the Chief Elected Officer

In an association with a balanced mode, the chief elected officer is the board chair and sets the board's agenda, presides over its meetings, guides its discussions, and discerns the climate for decisions. As chair, the chief elected officer is also the volunteer in closest daily contact with the CSE. The chief elected officer is in the best position to gauge board reactions to situations and can determine whether a matter merits board consideration, whether a poll of the board is sufficient, or whether the chief elected officer and the CSE together can first decide on a matter and subsequently report to the board. At the CSE's initiative the chief elected officer can and should advise the CSE on a wide variety of issues. The chief elected officer also usually has the jobs of appointing volunteer committees and their chairs, of carrying out ceremonial functions, and of serving as the primary spokesperson to the members, the public, and in tandem with the CSE, the government.

Relationship Between the Chief Elected Officer and Staff

As a rule, the chief elected officer and the volunteer leaders work through the CSE when making requests that involve any significant amount of staff time. The CSE's responsibility for staff is reinforced when the chief elected officer and other volunteer leaders work through him or her and is undercut when volunteers freely direct the staff.

Rigid adherence to this rule could create a bureaucracy, and so the CSE should ensure that the chief elected officer and other volunteer leaders have room to interact with the staff. In particular, the chief elected officer should be able to approach staff for information or to follow up on a request. It is also important that staff members know the chief elected officer and other volunteer leaders and their needs.

The Chief Staff Executive as CEO

A CSE often has a difficult time handling the role of a real chief executive officer (CEO). Decisions made in this capacity can cause trouble because they result in winners and losers among the members and the volunteer leaders. Volunteers may feel de-energized if they sense they have no real say in the direction of the association, and there may be rumblings about dictatorial leadership. Sooner or later, the CSE will make a decision that runs counter to the interests of some significant member segment. Faced with a choice between the CSE and the members, the board usually asks for the executive's resignation.

The Chief Elected Officer as CEO

When the chief elected officer attempts to function as a CEO, there can be unfortunate results. A chief elected officer who serves as part-time CEO is either too involved in or too removed from the day-to-day affairs of the association to function effectively. Striking a balance is difficult and made harder still if the chief elected officer also has a business to run or a profession to practice, as is frequently the case.

Some other consequences are discussed next.

- Substantial and usually excessive demands are made on an active chief elected officer, because this person is seen as the only significant decision maker.

- The staff never know precisely who is running the association —the chief elected officer or the CSE. To staff, it seems as if the chief elected officer can step in and take over any time, but, because this person is not always there, the CSE's authority is unclear.

- Life is difficult and sometimes unbearable for the CSE, who must pay close attention and conform to the chief elected officer's idea of what the association should do. This can lead to short-term staff activities that represent a significant drain on available resources. The CSE must always be wary that directions to staff may be countermanded.

- The association may be subjected to wide swings in programs and priorities as each new CEO attempts to make a lasting impression.

- The association is subjected to spotty extremes in leadership from an individual who holds office for a short time and who usually lacks sufficient perspective to make circumspect decisions.

- With so much power vested in the chief elected officer, other parts of the governance structure may become passive.

The Board as CEO

Particularly in associations with balanced staff and volunteer influence, the CEO function is a collective responsibility carried out by the board. The board holds the power that one normally ascribes to the CEO, that is, to make policy, set direction, make decisions, hire and fire the chief operating officer, and commit the organization financially and programmatically. Regardless of title, the association board (or the executive committee) performs the functions of the CEO, has more actual power than a corporate board, and does more work.[12]

In carrying out the CEO's function, the board is responsible for the following duties:

- supervising and directing the affairs of the association;

- approving the strategic plan;

- approving policies governing the effective and efficient use of human and financial resources;

- overseeing the finances, including preparation of the annual budget;

- hiring and evaluating the CSE's performance;

- reviewing and evaluating the work of committees and other volunteer groups;

- taking positions on issues of public policy affecting the industry or profession; and

- establishing membership criteria.

The board serves as a strong link in the association's chain of accountability between the operating units—staff and volunteer —and the members. It holds these units accountable and is in turn held accountable to the members via elections and reports.

Role of the Executive Committee

Associations frequently create an executive committee, accountable to the board, to handle the administrative oversight particularly if the board is too large to operate efficiently or to meet often enough to oversee activities. The board normally delegates to the executive committee the responsibility of overseeing the administration of the association between meetings of the board and providing guidance to the CSE. The executive committee of an association with a balanced mode would normally receive reports from the CSE (and other staff he or she designates) on the association's activities; review actual operating results against plans and budgets; handle policy issues, referring appropriate ones to the board; deal with immediate issues and problems brought to it by the CSE; and review personnel matters brought to it by the CSE.

Benefits

The CSEs surveyed cited as the principal benefits of an association with a balanced mode efficiency; stable, evenhanded, consistent, professional management; the ability to keep in touch with members' needs; and members' involvement. Efficiency and consistency are possible when staff handle administration and when operating decisions are not made by groups of volunteers. Staff operation permits employment of uniform controls and management techniques and taking of fast action when needed.

In the legislative arena, consistent staff involvement in the work is highly beneficial because it builds long-term working relationships with legislators and their staffs, a condition that is not possible with volunteers who bounce in and out. However, volunteer participation in the government affairs program is essential because it ensures that voters are heard and thus improves the image of the industry or profession.

Volunteer involvement builds interest and a sense of ownership and pride in members. It encourages broad-based advocacy of the association's goals and activities and expands the pool of capable and interested leaders. Many survey respondents reported that volunteer involvement makes the organization's activities more relevant to and better able to meet members' needs.

A balanced leadership mode avoids some pitfalls of staff-driven modes, such as staff remoteness from the needs of volunteers or day-to-day industry problems, staff defensiveness, and de-energized volunteers. It also transcends some drawbacks associated with a volunteer-driven mode, such heavy volunteer involvement in the association's daily affairs and the inefficiencies and uncertainties of relying on volunteers to perform much of the ongoing work.

Balance as a Strong Base for Leadership

Most associations can successfully lead their industry, profession, or cause by giving voice to issues that members face and setting forth ideas, guidelines, and standards that promote responsible action. Leadership is frequently needed in such areas as ethics, financial solvency, the environment, labor relations, education, safety, foreign competition, taxes, accounting, new technologies, product standards, and a host of others, many of which cannot be addressed by individual members and which require collective action.

By providing leadership, associations help to create a context that enables their industry, profession, or cause to grow and develop responsibly. The association of direct selling (door-to-door) firms, for example, aware that the industry was in jeopardy from some shady practices, created standards to make it harder for firms to gouge consumers. A 48-hour cooling-off period was established wherein a customer can return purchases; a fund was established to recoup the cost of complaints in case of bankruptcy; and a third-party due-process arrangement was instituted to handle conflicts between members and consumers.

Because of these changes, the industry has avoided much burdensome regulation and wide public disenchantment. Other groups that have assumed leadership roles include associations concerned with advertising, the health professions, and financial services—all have recognized problems facing their industries and professions and persuaded members to change their practices.

In other industries, however, associations have failed to provide needed leadership. For example, the nuclear power and electric utility industries did not acknowledge and deal early on with key issues such as safety, design standardization, radioactive waste storage, and operator training. As nuclear power became more common, opponents seized upon these issues, causing the construction of new nuclear power plants in the United States to come to a virtual standstill and putting existing facilities under pressure to shut down.

Part of what preoccupied this industry's associations and their leaders were short-term considerations, such as funding, avoiding restrictive regulation, labor problems, developing competitive edges for individual construction companies, and preempting competition from other fuel sources. These and similar problems must have made it difficult for the nuclear power and related associations to focus on longer-term, seemingly remote, and less urgent issues, such as safety, escalating construction costs, and waste disposal. These latter issues were downstream, deferrable, and possibly susceptible to handling by appropriate rate structures and guarantees. Anyone raising these issues in the associations may have run the risk of censure from other members for creating self-fulfilling prophecies, or stirring up problems.

Had the nuclear power industry, through its associations, dealt earlier and more directly with the issues by setting uniform standards for design, construction, and operation, for example, it is possible that nuclear power would today be a significantly larger factor in America's energy picture.

The same criticisms may be leveled at associations representing industries where foreign competition has encroached on or taken over U.S. markets because of technological superiority, ability to plan long term, and willingness to adapt to consumers' demands.

Exercising leadership is often difficult and risky for an association. It requires culling the issues, calling the most urgent ones to the attention of the industry or profession, proposing solutions, and enlisting the members' action. Although the proposed remedies may be in the long-term best interests of the larger industry or profession, they usually require at least some members to alter their behavior or accept limits on their freedom.

Thus, the best long-term strategy may conflict with short-term tactics, and in associations, short-term considerations often carry greater weight. Members may object to the association's heavy-handedness, which causes them to do things they would not do otherwise. Some may resign, and some may accuse the association of meddling. In all associations, there are people who do not want to think about the long term and whose horizons are limited. Indeed, some associations seem bent on excluding visionaries and statesmen. Yet, without leaders who can convince their associations to assume leadership roles in dealing with longer-term issues, frequently no one else will, except, perhaps, government agencies or Congress.

The fact is associations are well positioned to lead. Their leaders often draw from among the leaders in the industry, profession, or cause. Associations have the means to communicate directly with the entire industry, profession, or group most interested in the association's cause. They have the ability and the legitimacy to mount studies for use in framing issues and developing plans of action and can represent sufficient credibility to move their members.

An association's leadership credibility builds on its ability to influence the economic and social environment of its members. This ability flows from the following elements:

- A financial structure that is not overly dependent on the dues or contributions of a few key members; these members could discontinue membership with little penalty to the individuals but great penalty to the association;

- the efficient delivery of valued member services;

- a CSE and senior staff who have the support of volunteer leadership;

- organizational processes, including research, that highlight long-range issues and problems and permit an honest assessment of the future;

- a volunteer leadership structure capable of reviewing the entire industry, profession, or cause in order to formulate policy.

The staff have a stake in the long-term survival and growth of the association. Accordingly, it is in their best interests to be alert to trends and issues that threaten the health of the industry or profession and to ensure that those trends and issues are addressed. Volunteer leaders, too, must be able to confront issues from a long-term perspective and to promote practices conducive to the long-range economic interests of the members.

Thus, the process of formulating and communicating influential ideas requires input from *both* volunteers and staff. Volunteers are on the firing line. Because of their immersion in the industry, profession, or issue, they know what is possible and what is not, the costs and risks of responding to problems, the competitive implications of responses from one member segment but not from another. The formulation of issues and determination of association responses require member input.

The staff's expertise concerns how to put people together to formulate ideas and how best to package and communicate these. Staff know the consequences of giving voice to an idea or remaining silent and can anticipate responses depending on how the idea is presented, by whom, at what time, and in what forum. They know the financial implications of a move by the association in terms of dues and other revenue.

Leadership by an association requires a partnership of staff and volunteers. In an association that practices a balanced mode of operation, leadership is a natural byproduct that flows from established working relationships.

Chapter 9

Why Leadership Modes Shift

Why does an association shift its leadership mode? This chapter examines factors that cause shifts in leadership modes, based on opinions and experiences of chief staff executives (CSEs).

Why Associations Become Volunteer-Driven

Efforts by the Chief Staff Executive

The most frequently mentioned reason why organizations become more volunteer-driven is that the CSE seeks to increase volunteer participation. Among the associations that reported being more volunteer-driven today than ten years ago, 77 percent of the CSEs of trade and professional associations and 79 percent of the CSEs of philanthropic associations cited their own initiatives. Some respondents indicated that they were hired to increase volunteer participation.

Increased volunteer participation has been accomplished in many ways, including changing how the board conducts business, seeing that the board makes decisions, encouraging frequent volunteer consultations with elected officers, stimulating committees and committee chairs to take a more active role in policy formulation and backing them with staff support, involving volunteers in strategic planning and other pivotal activities, engaging volunteers in the search for new products and services, and surveying the members to learn their opinions about present and prospective activities of the association. These types of moves, supported by a CSE who seeks and welcomes the participation of volunteers in decision making, can significantly shift the leadership mode.

Changes in the Environment

The second major reason cited for a shift to a volunteer-driven mode is that conditions in the industry or profession change, spurring volunteers to take a more active interest in association affairs.

As a rule, members tend to be less active in the association when the industry or profession is growing, business is good, there are few perceived threats to the industry's or profession's viability, and the association seems to be functioning well. However, when the industry takes a downturn, a shake-out occurs, or the profession is threatened, particularly by the prospect of legislation or regulation, members tend to increase their activity and look to the association for answers. This is often the time when members scapegoat the association for failing to provide leadership, protection, services, support, and cost-effective programming. In response, volunteer leaders become more active and attempt to assert more control over association affairs.

Among the philanthropic associations, 36 percent cited changes in the members' environment as a reason behind a shift to a more volunteer-driven mode. These changes included fund-raising difficulty that required greater volunteer involvement, changing ethnic populations and service needs, increased competition for funds from other not-for-profit organizations, changes in life-styles (for example, fewer people who smoke), and, for one organization, a brighter financial picture that created greater volunteer interest.

New Breed of Member

The third most common reason in becoming more volunteer-driven is the emergence of volunteer leaders who want to be more active and who are unwilling to leave the management of the organization entirely to staff. The new volunteers may see the association as having significant untapped potential for delivering services or for shaping the environment of members. They may desire to sweep the place clean, revive what seems to be a sleepy organization, or take part for reasons of professional or personal advancement. Whatever the reasons, organizations that have shifted toward the volunteer-driven end of the spectrum have experienced a trend for newer, younger volunteers to become active in association affairs. This trend arises in trade, professional, and philanthropic associations alike. Among trade and professional associations, 42 percent of the CSEs surveyed cited such a new breed of member, and among philanthropic associations, 53 percent cited it.

Committee Influence

The fourth most common reason stems from volunteer committees that begin to exert more influence over the affairs of the association. As noted in chapter 6, the role of volunteer committees helps determine whether an association is volunteer- or staff-driven. A change in the way these committees function and their relationship to staff causes a shift in the balance of volunteer and staff direction.

Nearly 40 percent of the CSEs of associations of all types which have moved in a volunteer-driven direction indicated that volunteer committees are exerting greater influence over staff activities. In addition, more than 30 percent of the CSEs said that committees have more influence with the board.

Rejection of Staff Authority

In some cases, the chief elected officer with the support of the board moves to change the style of leadership by rejecting staff domination. If two or three chief elected officers in a row all see that volunteers have little say and no power and decide to do something about it, they can influence a significant shift.

A coup does not occur often in the life of an association. When it does, it is often characterized by anger and resentment, for a member faction usually sides with the CSE, preferring the status quo, and another faction allies itself with the insurgent leadership. If the CSE is reasonably flexible and has built support among the volunteers, he or she may be able to outlast the insurgency. However, when the transition is handled badly or when either the CSE or the new volunteer leaders polarize the situation, the result can split the membership and force the CSE's removal. A residue of hard feelings can last for years and the experience can color decisions in subsequent crises. In the extreme, some members form a new organization, with or without the CSE.

In many cases, a shift to more volunteer control lasts only a few years, until the volunteers who initiated the move leave office. This happens most frequently when the CSE remains in position despite the shift and the volunteers cannot devote sufficient time to running the association.

Crisis

During a crisis, volunteers frequently move in to take control. The problems may be financial, such as a string of deficits or a costly error in judgment, or managerial, such as a staff exodus, serious staff complaints, or poor performance. When the problems obviously start to affect the association's ability to function, the situation can become unstable.

Often, the volunteers work strenuously to change the CSE's behavior. If these efforts do not succeed and the CSE is not removed immediately, the volunteer leaders may take charge. They may want to sign all checks, meet with staff department heads to review operations, require development of written goals and timetables, and meet more frequently than usual with the CSE. All of these measures have the effect of moving the volunteers closer to the operations of the association and reducing the CSE's power and authority.

In most cases, the crisis lasts only until the CSE makes sufficient changes to put the association back on course or a new CSE is found. When the situation returns to near normal, the volunteers ordinarily withdraw and the former pattern of staff-volunteer relations reasserts itself. As one CSE put it, "Five years ago, a previous chief staff executive mismanaged the organization. Three years ago, the organization became totally volunteer-driven for approximately 18 months. Now, the association is back to being mostly staff-driven" (8 on a scale of 9).

Strategic Planning

In philanthropic associations that have shifted toward a volunteer-driven mode, 55 percent of the CSEs cited strategic planning as a primary reason. Two-thirds of the philanthropic associations with a volunteer-driven or balanced mode indicated that the strategic planning process increased volunteer influence, as did 44 percent of the staff-driven associations.

Among all trade and professional associations, 43 percent said that strategic planning increased volunteer influence to some extent, and 28 percent attributed their shift specifically to strategic planning. These CSEs felt that the planning process exposed the volunteers involved to the functioning of the organization, enabling them to take a more active role as board members or committee chairs.

Many of the same CSEs who said that strategic planning increased the influence of the volunteers also said that it increased the influence of the staff. Planning, then, broadened the influence of the leadership.

Additional Funds for the Volunteer Structure

An increase in funds to support the volunteer structure was cited as an impetus in becoming more volunteer-driven by 20 percent of the philanthropic associations and 12 percent of the trade and professional associations. This assessment is supported by other survey responses which indicate that in volunteer-driven associations, committee members' expenses are reimbursed significantly more often than in staff-driven associations (see chapter 4).

Why Associations Become Staff-Driven

Staff Professionalism

Increased professionalism of staff was by far the most frequent reason given for associations to become more staff-driven. Ninety-one percent of the CSEs of philanthropic associations and 78 percent of the CSEs of trade and professional associations cited this major cause.

In the association world, continued emphasis has been put on staff training and education to handle the increased technical complexity of association work. The American Society of Association Executives (ASAE), the U.S. Chamber of Commerce, and large philanthropic associations such as the YMCA and Scouts all have active training programs. ASAE, alone and in conjunction with the University of Maryland, sponsors seminars and courses and publishes materials on general association management and specialty areas, such as meeting planning, marketing, financial management, association law, and non-dues income.

Hand in hand with the increasing complexity and technical content of association activities go changes in the expectations of staff. Member companies have sophisticated expectations of their trade associations; professional society members demand better and more knowledgeable performance; philanthropic association volunteers expect professional support in their fund-raising efforts and require more professional administration of association affairs.

These forces combine to upgrade the level of professional expertise available to and used by associations. While volunteer guidance and direction are still sought and desired even in the most technical areas, the opinions of staff are increasingly deferred to. It is difficult, for example, for volunteers who oversee the educational programs to ignore the recommendations of an education staffer concerning the mode and content of seminar programs when the staffer's background and experience outdistance those of the volunteers.

As the field of association management expands and becomes more technical, staff influence grows and shifts the character of the whole association toward the staff-driven mode.

Technology

An increase in the technical content of the association's activities was given as a reason for becoming more staff-driven by 54 percent of philanthropic associations and 37 percent of trade and professional associations. The introduction of the microcomputer has been a significant factor, enabling sophisticated products and technical analysis, particularly in such areas as publishing, meetings and conventions management, education, and standards setting. Competition in the association world has increased the complexity of meeting planning, negotiating with hotels and convention facilities, developing educational offerings, lobbying, and other activities. With complexity comes the need for expertise and experience in the areas mentioned, and most volunteers have neither. Thus, the tasks and, by extension, their direction have devolved increasingly to the full-time staff.

Changes in the Board

Fifty-seven percent of the CSEs of trade and professional associations and 52 percent of those of philanthropic associations reported that a change in their boards from serving as a management committee to functioning as a policy group was a major factor in their becoming more staff-driven.

A board that functions as a management committee concerns itself with the management and administration of the association to include budget details, personnel decisions, programmatic adjustments, program direction, and the like. A policy board concerns itself with the overall direction of the association and establishment of member-related and legislative policy.

A board that functions as a management committee often comprises the chairs of the key operating committees, plus the elected officers, and perhaps some regional representatives. Thus, the chairs of committees on membership, chapter affairs, publications, public relations, government affairs, standards, research, and the like sit on the board by virtue of their positions. These operating committee chairs frequently oversee parts of the association's budget, including staff departments.

Management committee boards, as a rule, concentrate proportionately more on the activities of particular segments of the association with which board members are familiar and proportionately less on issues facing the association as a whole. This micromanagement places the volunteers in a stronger position to initiate and shape the activities of the association, and therefore to drive it, than if the board concentrates its attention on overall policy and finances.

Policy boards more often comprise members elected at large. If representatives of operational components do sit on the board, the agenda can be arranged so that policy and directional matters receive top priority and the most time. Policy boards, as a rule, concentrate proportionately more on issues facing the association and its industry, profession, or cause and proportionately less on administrative matters or individual association segments.

Procedural changes on boards also have propelled shifts to a staff-driven mode. Removing administrative matters from board agendas, adopting consent agendas or consent calendars, and in other ways streamlining board activities have reduced the time spent on routine administration and with it volunteer involvement in administrative affairs.

Changes in Committees

A change in the role of committees from directing to advising staff was given as a reason for becoming more staff-driven by 47 percent of the philanthropic associations and 34 percent of the trade and professional associations. (Also see chapter 4.) Sometimes committees explicitly are renamed as advisory committees; other times, committee charters are changed. The result in each case is to reduce the volunteers' influence in operational matters and to increase the staff's authority and latitude.

Nondues Income

An increase in nondues income was given by 45 percent of the trade and professional associations and 31 percent of the philanthropic associations as a reason for becoming more staff-driven. Activities that generate nondues income require a relatively high degree of expertise more compatible with staff management and direction than with volunteer leadership.

Strategic Planning

Paradoxically, strategic planning can increase staff influence in the association, as well as volunteer influence. Among staff-driven trade and professional associations that engage in strategic planning, 64 percent said the planning process strengthened staff influence. In staff-driven philanthropic associations, 54 percent reported an increase in staff influence from strategic planning.

It is probable that the planning process used in these associations had heavy staff representation and input, and in some cases the process may have been carried out entirely by staff. Where there was volunteer input, indications are that the influence of staff and volunteers was increased.

New Breed of Member

Approximately 40 percent of all respondents whose associations had become more staff-driven spoke of the existence of a new breed of member who is not as interested in driving the association as members in years past. In some cases, business owners had been replaced by professional managers who viewed the association in different terms than their predecessors. While the old guard members looked on the association as theirs and as a place to meet informally with peers, the new breed is less interested in social aspects, identifies less intensely with the organization, and is more interested in government affairs, taxation, and other matters affecting their business.

This new breed has less time to spend on association business than their predecessors. Corporate executives are in heavy demand to serve on a variety of boards, corporate and nonprofit. Little time is available to serve the association actively. Many corporate CEOs use as stand-ins deputies who are even less committed and more reluctant to get involved in the day-to-day affairs of the association.

Some associations reported that, because of deregulation, competition among member companies has increased, causing volunteers to look to their companies' needs rather than to the needs of the association or to the comradeship they might gain from association meetings.

A few respondents said that company cutbacks reduced the number of people available for association work on committees and in technical areas, such as data processing, law, and marketing. To cope, the association had to take on additional staff, who assumed the functions once performed by volunteers.

Role of the Chief Staff Executive

Thirty-five percent of the CSEs of trade and professional associations and 27 percent of those of philanthropic associations indicated that they were hired to make the association more staff-directed. The result of this mandate, whether explicit or inferred, was that these executives felt justified and supported in taking more control of the staff and the affairs of the association.

Number of Volunteer Committees

About 10 percent of the respondents said that their associations were more staff-driven because the number of volunteer committees had been reduced, thereby reducing the degree of volunteer oversight of the staff.

Experiences of Chief Staff Executives

Case Study 1: Volunteer Expulsion of the Chief Staff Executive

In a national trade association, a CSE was hired to provide strong leadership to the staff and the association—in essence, to make the association more staff-driven. The search committee was composed largely of past presidents who wanted a forceful leader who could consistently represent the association in government circles. The new executive's credentials were impressive: a doctorate, extensive experience as the second in command in another large trade organization, and time in government service at senior policy levels.

The executive consolidated his power and over the course of about 18 months assumed many of the decision-making functions once done by the officers and the board. Although he attempted to keep the volunteer leaders informed, there were several instances where he made significant decisions without their consultation. In other cases, the board approved programs that the CSE initiated but with only minimal understanding of the implications for staffing and impact on member services.

In the transitional process, the CSE, who referred to his mandate, was somewhat heavy-handed. He alienated several volunteer leaders, none of whom were on his search committee. By the end of his second year, he was seen by many (although not a majority) of the volunteer leaders as arrogant, uncommunicative, and too powerful.

The volunteer leaders tolerated the CSE for several more years, despite increasing grumbling among their ranks and other parts of the membership. Then a serious problem was discovered with a newly installed computer system: Both the capital and operating costs were significantly higher than original estimates. The board was unprepared for the negative impact on the financial operating statement.

About the same time, a young, new president was elected. The computer problem catalyzed the feelings of the volunteers who had felt left out and, shortly afterward, the CSE was removed. A new CSE was brought in who was more comfortable with volunteer involvement and whose skills and capabilities were known to the volunteer leadership.

Case Study 2: A Chief Elected Officer as CEO

In a medium-size trade association whose members are small businesses, a newly installed chief elected officer attempted to take over as CEO, as permitted in the bylaws. Although the volunteer leadership had historically been passive, the new president felt that the staff was too content with the status quo and negative to new proposals. To initiate a change, the elected president began a strategic planning process and appointed himself chair of the strategic planning committee.

As part of the planning process, he conducted a series of meetings with the volunteer leaders and staff, during which he encouraged criticism of the organization, its operation, and management. He also forced the hiring of a new staff member, a vice president of marketing, over the objections of the CSE, and he instituted a process whereby the volunteer leaders set objectives for the CSE to meet. His actions left the organization in turmoil, with the staff confused about who was running the association.

Succeeding presidents carried on some of the activities initiated by the activist president, so the leadership culture was altered, at least for a few years. Gradually, however, the planning process atrophied and the association reverted to being staff-driven, although not to the previous degree. The CSE's job was never in serious jeopardy, because he did not actively fight the moves of the president but, rather, went along. The marketing vice president left within four years and was not replaced.

Case Study 3: Volunteer Initiative for a Staff-Driven Mode

In a third association, which had for years been volunteer-driven, the volunteer leaders decided that more staff direction was needed to deal with staff morale problems and to permit the association to grow. The existing CSE had been selected principally because his personality meshed with an extremely volunteer-driven association. He was unassertive and did not challenge the activities of volunteers, despite some serious budget problems caused by mid-year program changes that committee members made and forced through the board.

Volunteer leaders worked with the CSE for about a year, encouraging him to be more active and assertive. Although there was some progress, the volunteers finally gave up, the CSE was asked to retire early, and a new, tougher manager was hired. The association is still largely volunteer-driven, but the new CSE has taken greater control of the staff, set limits on volunteer direction of the staff, and established conformance to annual budgets set by the board. The volunteer leaders seem happy with the changes and comfortable that the association is operating in a sound manner.

Case Study 4: A Chief Staff Executive's Initiative for a Staff-Driven Mode

The CSE of a professional society has moved over the past five years to make the organization more staff-driven. He has actively discouraged the formation of counterpart volunteer committees to oversee the staff; has consistently worked to upgrade the staff's professionalism by hiring experts in marketing, program development, publications, and education; and has encouraged staff to take outside training in their specialties. He and the staff have developed new products and services to increase the association's income, decrease the percentage of income from dues, and make the association function more like a business.

During this time, the volunteers have either acquiesced or actively supported his moves in the belief that staff should run the association and volunteers should direct it. In fact, the staff not only run, but also largely direct this association. The CSE is happy with what he has done, and is now looking for a more challenging situation.

Case Study 5: A Chief Staff Executive's Initiative for a Volunteer-Driven Mode

A national association of state and local government agencies had historically been run by the headquarters staff, with little volunteer say on priorities, direction, or programs. Paid staff of affiliated state associations, moreover, were able to limit the scope of the national association's activities because of their influence with state representatives who served on the board of the national association. They counseled their representatives to resist any attempt by the national association to expand.

To reduce the stranglehold of the state association executives, the national CSE took a series of steps aimed at strengthening the role of the volunteer leaders by encouraging them to function more as national directors and less as state representatives to the national board. He initiated a long-range strategic planning process that involved the board and increased communication to the board and committee chairs about the national association's finances, problems, and needs. He also increased financial and staff support of volunteer activities, including conferences and regional meetings, and created a senior staff position for the state association liaison.

These moves increased the volunteers' awareness and interest and helped them to approach the national-state relationship in a more relaxed fashion. Volunteers now have a greater say in the direction of the association, and the board has permitted the organization to expand in ways that would have been impossible a few years ago.

Chapter 10

Strategies for Shifting Leadership Modes

I n the life of most associations, there comes a time when the leadership mode needs to shift. Some associations need to become more staff-driven in order to grow, achieve more efficient operations, develop more continuity in programs, or take new initiatives. Others need to become more volunteer-driven in order to strengthen the connection with the members, energize them, gain greater member participation, better discern members' needs, or heighten awareness of what is going on in the field. Still others need a better balance between staff and volunteers to free energies wasted in internal conflicts over influence. Whether the impetus for the change arises from the chief staff executive (CSE), the volunteer leaders, a committee, or some factor outside the association, the CSE must usually manage the transition.[13]

The CSE may take over an association already in transition or receive a new challenge to shift leadership modes in response to volunteer pressure, a strategic plan, external forces, growth, or other factors. Other high-level executives in the association may also need to participate in a transition.

Minimizing Risks

Changing the relationships in an association, particularly those between volunteers and staff, involves risk. Staff and volunteers alike who are accustomed to the status quo and believe that it is satisfactory normally resist efforts to change. Some perceive change as a threat to their prerogatives, territory, or influence; others fear the unknown; still others fear a loss of value in their skills and experience. Some staff may seize upon change as a chance to redress old grievances, particularly those who harbor ill will against the CSE.

Minimizing risk requires a plan for making the change, as well as trust and communication. By being explicit about the need for and dimensions of the change with volunteer leaders and staff, the CSE can build the essential base of trust needed to proceed satisfactorily. Attempting surreptitiously to shift the locus of influence will likely cause a negative reaction. Both staff and volunteers are sensitive to the issue of influence and will detect a shift, particularly when their control diminishes.

So, a clear rationale for the change should preface any effort to alter the style of an organization, that is, why must things be done differently? A case should buttress the need for change by showing how and why the association is not meeting its potential or what difficulty it may face in the future. For example, in small associations that have the potential for growth, the need may be apparent for more staff implementation of board decisions because the volunteers cannot continue to carry out the increasing work. In larger, more established associations, the need may not be so clear, and other reasons must be brought into play.

Gaining the concurrence of volunteer leaders is not always easy. Frank discussions with elected leaders, the executive committee, and the board help to solidify the rationale and secure agreement about the steps to be taken. To ensure a smooth transition from one leadership mode to another, volunteers need to understand that it is in their long-term best interests to shift the locus of influence.

The staff, too, should discuss the benefits and drawbacks of a shift and its potential effect on relationships with volunteers, on the task of serving volunteer committees, on their workload, and so forth. Obtaining the staff's understanding and commitment are also important in gaining general agreement among volunteer leaders and in implementing the shift.

It is usually easier for the CSE to secure the volunteers' agreement to shift to a more volunteer-driven mode than a staff-driven one. That is because people resist giving up something and answering to another who holds their relinquished control. Volunteers may charge the CSE with building a bureaucracy if he or she seeks to make the association more staff-driven. Thus, in such instances it is helpful to have a volunteer present the case to other volunteers. Consultants also can be valuable in developing the rationale and plan for change and in guiding the process.

Regardless of the type of change sought, the CSE must exercise care to distinguish between causes and effects. For example, a volunteer-driven association has certain characteristics, such as a larger governing board, that distinguish it from a staff-driven association. However, simply increasing the size of the board may do little or nothing to make the association more volunteer-driven, because board size can be a byproduct of or unrelated to the leadership mode.

What strategies, then, are available to CSEs and volunteer leaders who want or need to shift the leadership mode of their organization? The strategies explored next have worked for various association executives or bear support from the survey data. Speculative strategies are identified as such. (Also see chapter 4, "Correlating Factors.")

Strategies for a More Volunteer-Driven Mode

Empower the Board

A board can be empowered by increasing its decision-making capability and its focus on decisions that direct the course of the association. The board agenda is key to increasing decision-making capability. The CSE and board chair together can fashion agendas for board meetings that seek action on the allocation of human and financial resources and that call for policy decisions to guide specific staff and committee actions. In preparing an agenda, the CSE and chief elected officer should first agree on the results desired from the board meeting and then order the items and determine the time to be allocated to each. Individual board members may then be lined up to propose motions, support positions, and contribute to discussion.

Careful agenda preparation can transform a board from a reactive, report-receiving body to an active, decision-making one, thus profoundly increasing volunteer direction in the association. The results may include greater commitment of time and energy from board members, increased attendance at meetings, and a sense among the volunteers that they have more influence in the association.

Create an Executive Committee

The majority of associations have executive committees, but volunteer-driven associations employ them more often than staff-driven associations. If the association has a fairly large board (at least 15 members) and no executive committee, then establishing an executive committee can help to shift the leadership mode. By meeting frequently with the CSE and dealing with program, budget, and personnel matters, the volunteers on the executive committee can direct the association's affairs.

The executive committee should meet regularly between meetings of the board (not just before board meetings) and handle administrative and operational matters that do not need to take up the board's time. Reports of executive committee actions should be made at each board meeting and actions requiring board consideration placed on the board agenda.

Increase Volunteer Decision Making

The degree of volunteer participation in decision-making processes is significant in determining whether an association is volunteer-driven or staff-driven. It also forms the basis of the most successful strategy for making associations more volunteer-driven.

CSEs may employ a variety of methods to boost the involvement of volunteers in the association's decision processes. For example, CSEs may include action items on the agendas of operating committees to encourage more significant decisions, to force confrontation with issues facing the association and its components, and to reduce information-gathering sessions. Committee chairs can be trained in meetings management. The committee staff liaison and committee chair can determine desired outcomes of committee meetings in advance and prepare agendas accordingly. The CSE can solicit in advance the advice of the chief elected officer and other officers on decisions and ask the chief elected officer to make decisions more often.

Form Counterpart Committees or
Increase Their Staff Direction

Volunteer-driven associations of all kinds embody more structural congruence between staff departments and volunteer committees than staff-driven associations. Counterpart committees permit volunteers to oversee and become involved in the activities of specific staff departments, and contribute to volunteer direction of the association. Counterpart committees are particularly appropriate in areas such as education, field services, chapter affairs, and industry or professional activities.

The counterpart committees of volunteer-driven associations direct staff activities much more often than those of staff-driven associations. To increase their direction of staff a threefold strategy is indicated. First, amend the charters of counterpart committees to enable their giving direction to the staff in such areas as project and program development and budget preparation. The counterpart committee can also assume a role in an annual evaluation of departmental activities.

Second, direct staff who serve counterpart committees to work with their committee chairs to formulate explicit annual goals. The most productive goal-setting processes involve four persons, according to the survey respondents: the committee chair, the staffer serving the committee, the CSE, and the chief elected officer. The latter two need not be present at meetings when goals are set. The process requires the CSE and chief elected officer (together, perhaps, with the board or executive committee) to formulate general committee goals that further overall association goals. Committee staffers and chairs then hold formal goal-setting sessions to set committee objectives for the coming year and timetables. These goals serve as the framework for the committee's work and as a means for evaluating its performance.

Third, require the committees to recommend policy and program changes to the board.

Thus, the influence of the volunteers grows and the association becomes more volunteer-driven. The paradox is that this strategy requires a more active staff as well.

Encourage Contested Elections

Contested elections for the chief elected officer, properly conducted, engage the members' attention and require candidates to voice their ideas about association priorities and possible future direction, thereby influencing the association.

Changing from uncontested to contested elections is a strategy appropriate for associations that have an adequate pool of prospective candidates; otherwise, contested elections are not feasible. This move usually requires amending the bylaws or constitution.

Strengthen the Accountability of the Chief Staff Executive to the Chief Elected Officer

Although most CSEs are accountable directly to the board, in volunteer-driven associations the chief elected officer holds more authority in the chain of accountability than in staff-driven associations. Naming the chief elected officer as the primary point of accountability for the CSE strengthens the volunteer-driven mode.

Develop a Strategic Plan

The understanding gained by volunteers during a strategic planning process augments their capacity to influence the association long after the planning process has been completed. Board members included on the planning committee are able to use insights gained during the planning process to more effectively govern the association. Furthermore, succeeding generations of volunteer leaders are often drawn from the ranks of the planning committee.

Increase Funding to the Volunteer Structure

Funding of volunteers' travel, meals, and meeting expenses makes it more possible for them to meet and the committee structure to work. Funding also is tangible evidence that the association welcomes the input of volunteers. The strategy, therefore, is to press for budgetary increases of items that support the operations of the volunteer structure.

Create a Delegate Assembly

While a radical strategy, forming a delegate assembly would make the association more volunteer-driven. Volunteer-driven associations have delegate assemblies much more often than staff-driven associations. Delegate assemblies represent an important source of volunteer influence and control in associations, although they are more difficult to manage than boards. Delegate assemblies often have the power to make resolutions that bind their associations, particularly concerning budgets, policies, and stands on national issues. Many delegate assemblies elect the boards of their associations, in whole or in part, and thus serve as a point of accountability for the board and executive committee.

The initiative for such a move, whether the volunteers', or the CSE's, needs the support of a careful study of the association's governance, including the implications of an assembly for the board, for costs, and for the membership.

Strategies for a More Staff-Driven Mode

Increase Staff Professionalism

Professionalizing the staff involves training existing staff and hiring specialists in such areas as meetings management, exhibit sales, marketing, and communications. Given budget limitations and normal staff turnover, this is a long-term strategy. If pursued consistently, it results in a more staff-driven association, because volunteers are more willing to look to a highly professional staff for direction, new program ideas, and expertise.

Change the Board's Character

Changing their boards from management committees to policy boards is a major factor in associations' becoming more staff-driven.

To change the character of the board a two-pronged strategy is indicated. First, balance with directors at large any operating committee chairs on the board whose presence focuses the board's work on components of the association rather than the association as a whole. Attempt to shift their role from that of committee chairs to liaisons to committees.

Second, refocus the board's attention more on policy and direction and less on administration. Doing this is facilitated if the CSE works closely with the board chair well in advance of meetings to design the board's agendas and determine desired outcomes.

Uncouple Volunteer Committees from Staff

In most staff-driven associations, the volunteer committee structure does not mirror the staff structure. The involvement of volunteers in staff activities can be reduced by establishing volunteer committees that do not parallel staff departments; by shifting the charters of counterpart committees so that they are broader, narrower, or otherwise different in scope from the staff departments; and by phasing out other counterpart committees. These changes will also reduce overall volunteer direction in the association.

New committees established in pursuit of this strategy should be assigned staff support in accordance with the association's normal policies. This strategy can be implemented over several years and must have the support of the volunteer leadership.

Create Advisory Committees

Changing the role of committees from directing to advising the staff was a reason for becoming more staff-driven in nearly half of the philanthropic associations and more than one-third of the trade and professional associations surveyed. The effect is to increase the authority and latitude of staff members.

A change to advisory status can be accomplished in many ways, including amending the charges to committees, creating advisory committees alongside more directive committees, or even amending the bylaws. More common are informal changes, such as brainstorming during committee meetings to generate ideas for staff, focusing the committee on problem solving rather than administrative matters, eliminating committee review of departmental budgets, requiring staff to prepare committee agendas, and having staff report committee activities to the board instead of the committee chairs.

Increase the Technical Content and Complexity of the Work

As the body of experience in each area of association management grows and becomes more technical, the influence of the staff grows as well. Complexity is increasing because of the addition of revenue-producing services and programs and attempts to make existing activities, such as government and legal affairs, more effective.

The use of computers permits the sophisticated manipulation of information and increases the scope and efficiency of such functions as convention management, marketing, government affairs, membership development and tracking, publications, communications with members, internal accounting, and assembly of information on the industry or profession.

The strategy is to seek out and incorporate ways to increase the technical content and complexity of the association's work, thereby necessitating greater staff input and influence. This can be done by expanding the use of computers, tying into data bases, scheduling and planning events farther into the future, systematizing activities such as legislative tracking, adopting electronic publishing methods, conducting membership surveys on the value and use of association services, and employing other sophisticated operational techniques.

Cut Back Volunteer Committees

By reducing the number of volunteer committees and thus committee oversight, staff may devote more time to other matters. This is also a cost-saving move for those associations which reimburse committee members' expenses.

Eliminating a volunteer committee can be risky and requires the support of volunteer leaders. Risks can be reduced if committee disestablishment is supported by a sunset policy in which committees automatically dissolve after a specified period.

Develop Sources of Nondues Income

The survey data show that an increase in nondues income serves to make an association more staff-driven and that nondues income-producing activities are more staff-driven than other association member services.

Increase the Tenure of Board Members

Board members of staff-driven associations serve almost a year longer, on average, than those of volunteer-driven associations. To test whether this fact is a cause or an effect of the staff-driven mode, the subject was explored in interviews with CSEs. From this investigation, it was concluded that increased length of board service does have some effect on leadership mode. Board service beyond about three years seems to engender comfort and familiarity with the CSE and other senior staff. Board members with longer service appear to be more willing to let the CSE and staff run the show than board members who have held their positions two or three years.

The data are not conclusive but suggest that a strategy to increase the tenure of board members by as much as a year may result in increased staff influence.

Implementation requires increasing the number of terms that a board member may serve or increasing the length of the director's term of office (the average is 2.6 years for trade and professional associations and 2.7 years for philanthropic associations).

Negotiate an Employment Contract

Among trade and professional associations, more CSEs in staff-driven associations have employment contracts than in volunteer-driven associations. In contract negotiations, the CSE's responsibilities and authority are often spelled out. In order to attract and hold good people, the volunteer leaders may extend to a prospective executive significant authority, particularly in the staff management area. The terms of the contract can support the CSE in setting limits on volunteers' involvement in administration.

Require On-Call Executive Committee Meetings

Requiring fewer regular meetings of the executive committee and more on an on-call basis may make the association more staff-driven. Such a move reduces administrative oversight by volunteer leaders and the time spent by the chief elected officer on association business. If the executive committee meets at the CSE's request, it does so largely on the CSE's terms and takes up matters that the CSE has determined, resulting in increased staff direction.

The CSE may facilitate this strategy by requesting special meetings of the executive committee that, over time, supplant its regular meetings.

Chapter 11

Characteristics of Successful Chief Staff Executives

The chief staff executives (CSEs) of staff- and volunteer-driven associations differ significantly in how they approach their jobs and in their relationships with volunteer leaders. A recent unpublished study found that the CSEs of volunteer-driven associations focus their energy and attention inside the association—on the staff and on maintaining good relationships with the board.[14] CSEs of staff-driven associations, in contrast, focus on concerns outside the association—in the legislative and regulatory realm, on representing the association to the public, and on providing information to the members.[15]

In the study, the CSEs of member-driven associations ranked the following responsibilities significantly more important than the CSEs of staff-driven associations:

- delegating responsibilities, assigning and directing staff work, with appropriate follow-up and control;

- maintaining a positive work environment;

- working to develop rapport with staff;

- determining the causes of staff dissatisfaction and working to correct them;

- collaborating with the board, executive committee, and other designated entities in developing short- and long-range plans;

- understanding that good ideas are sometimes rejected.[16]

The CSEs of staff-driven associations rated the following factors significantly higher than those of member-driven associations:

- being an effective public speaker;
- maintaining good relationships with legislative and regulatory decision makers;
- serving as the spokesperson for the industry or profession;
- establishing a position on the major philosophical issues in the association;
- keeping members informed of significant legislative and regulatory initiatives;
- summarizing and disseminating comprehensive and reliable information on matters of interest to members;
- recommending to the board and finance committee priorities for proposed goals and programs.[17]

In Staff-Driven Associations

The CSEs of staff-driven associations view the association as theirs. Efficiency and getting work done are high priorities. They embody vision—what the association is all about and its direction. They know they have to gain the approval of volunteer leaders to mount significant initiatives and view that as necessary to do business. These CSEs view themselves as responsible for the functioning of the entire association, including the staff and the volunteer structures. Accordingly, they are active in selecting committee chairs and committee members and are highly participatory in board meetings, proposing items for board consideration, commenting on pending board action, offering opinions on issues facing the association, and otherwise exerting their influence. In cases where their role is not so visible, these CSEs still take an active hand in preparing board agendas and in briefing the board chair about issues that may arise and votes needed.

The CSEs of staff-driven association are frequently more isolated from volunteer leaders than the CSEs in volunteer-driven association, because they lack incentive to learn the priorities of each incoming president and to build a close working relationship.

Often, these CSEs are experts about the industry or profession of the association. This knowledge is a necessity if the CSEs are to be effective spokespersons who testify before Congress and represent the industry or profession to regulatory bodies. They may draw on the time and expertise of members for these representational tasks, and may even take a backseat to the chief elected officer. Even so, the CSEs provide the basic continuity in staff-driven associations.

In Volunteer-Driven Associations

CSEs of volunteer-driven associations have a clear, strong philosophy that volunteers must direct the assocation and that staff support the volunteers and handle the administrative tasks that facilitate volunteer participation and direction. They tend not to serve as spokespersons, leaving that job to the volunteer leaders, aided, perhaps, by the association's professional lobbyist. They tend not to be highly visible in the association or to the outside world.

The CSEs of volunteer-driven associations view their organizations as belonging to the members and their surrogates, the volunteer leaders. They see their jobs in narrower terms than the CSEs of staff-driven associations: They are responsible for the functioning of staff. As one executive put it, "I am charged with managing the staff of the association. The volunteer leaders run the volunteer structure—the committees and councils. I provide support to the volunteer structure but the volunteers are responsible for running it." Nonetheless, they are in close communication with the chief elected officer, conferring about problems and obtaining decisions or backing when dealing with operational and member-related problems.

In Associations with a
Balanced Leadership Mode

The CSEs of associations with a balanced leadership mode incorporate attributes of CSEs from staff-driven and volunteer-driven associations. They understand that the members own the association and that the CSE must share the role of spokesperson with the volunteer leaders to enhance the association's credibility.

These CSEs assume responsibility for the functioning of the entire association, recognizing that the staff largely determine the effectiveness of the committee structure in setting goals, providing information, and carrying out committee work. The CSEs frequently recommend policy to the board, either directly or through the elected officers, and take an active role in board discussions as experts in association management.

The CSEs of associations with a balanced mode view their position as a partnership with the volunteer leaders, with a major task being to maintain that partnership.

Chapter 12

Outlook for the Future

Based on trends of the past decade, it is possible to speculate about the evolution of leadership modes in associations over the next five to ten years and to discuss the underlying factors that will shape those modes.

Associations Will Become More Staff-Driven

The trend to become more staff-driven, seen clearly during the past ten years, will continue as associations grow and become more complex in their organization and operations and more professional in their staffing. Associations that are currently volunteer-driven will experience the most dramatic shift. Those that currently function with a balanced mode will also become more staff-driven.

In particular, professional societies and trade associations comprising individual members will become more staff-driven as they increase their political roles and need more expert lobbying. Philanthropic associations that depend on large individual contributions will shift the least toward the staff-driven mode, because their fund-raising imperatives will tend to hold them in place. Philanthropic associations that turn to special events for income will tend to become more staff-driven.

Staff executives will continue to seek education and training, as the pace of change accelerates and as their operations become more bottom-line oriented and computer based. New techniques for managing and delegating, particularly regarding volunteers, will be employed. Executives will strive to meet higher performance standards.

As their professionalism increases, so will the influence that executives wield in their associations. They will more often initiate and shape policies and new programs. Increasingly, the volunteer leaders will look to staff as principal decision makers in the organization.

The scope of the chief staff executive's (CSE's) responsibility will be accepted as encompassing the volunteer and staff structures. Boards will look to CSEs as their principal agents, responsible for carrying out directives by using all of the resources available to the association. The traditional notion that the CSE is responsible for the staff structure and the chief elected officer for the volunteer structure will gradually give way to the concept that the CSE is responsible for the whole organization.

The productivity of volunteer committees, in particular, will fall to the CSE as the person who directs the staff assigned to committees. The quality and level of staff support, as a rule, are major determinants of how well committees perform.

Chief Elected Officers Will Function as Board Chairs

The role of the chief elected officer will, more and more, be seen as that of the board chair, who is responsible for conducting board meetings and conferring with the CSE between meetings about items to bring before the board or executive committee. There will be less emphasis on the chief elected officer as the CSE's boss. The ceremonial duties will continue, but the operational role will diminish.

Titles Will Change

Over the next decade, more CSEs will carry the titles of president or executive vice president and more chief elected officers the title of chairman. This reflects a shift in responsibilities and roles and awareness that the CSE is responsible for the operation of the entire organization and the chief elected officer for the conduct of the board and executive committee.

Titles for the CSE have evolved over the years in a fashion analogous to titles in the hospital field. In hospitals, the chief staff executive was originally designated the superintendent of nursing, with that title later progressing to superintendent, administrator, and executive vice president. Now, it is common for the chief administrative officer to carry the title of president. Similarly, in associations, the CSE's original title was secretary or corresponding secretary, changing, as the field advanced, to executive secretary, executive director, and executive vice president. It is not unusual for the CSE to carry the title of president, particularly in trade associations. This trend will continue, reflecting the development of association management as a profession and the CSE's growing influence.

Operations Will Be More Businesslike

Continued development of nondues income sources, coupled with increased staff specialization and professionalism, will cause associations to function in a more businesslike manner. There will be more internal controls over costs, more detailed reporting of operations to the board, more emphasis on efficiency to conserve revenue, and greater attention to the bottom line. New program decisions will be based more on market and member research than in the past and will involve comparisons of projected revenues with initial investments required to generate those revenues.

Nondues income-generating activities will increase, despite attempts from the small business community to limit competition from nonprofit organizations. The prospect of net revenues with which to fund other desirable association activities and the use of computer technology will drive decisions to develop additional sources of income. Associations will be seen as collectors and purveyors of information of all kinds.

As associations continue to become more businesslike, they will also become more staff-driven. The pace of operation will be too rapid and continuity too vital to permit volunteer control of decisions and operations.

Governing Units Will Change

Driven by strategic planning and the need for greater productivity, associations will assess the efficiency of their volunteer and staff structures and processes and weigh the balance between volunteer and staff influence. Governing boards that operate as management committees will give way to policy boards. Large, unwieldy boards will form executive committees to handle administrative oversight; these committees will perform an advisory function to CSEs. Boards that are too large to function in a decision-making capacity will evolve into delegate assemblies with the power to approve budgets, pass resolutions, and elect some members of the board.

There will be increased use of combination staff-volunteer management committees to make decisions. Management committees, comprising the CSE, legal counsel, a government affairs staffer, and the top two elected officers, for example, can meet on short notice, operate efficiently, and prevent delays that would otherwise occur were the association relying on a board or executive committee for decisions. Gradually, management committees will augment or replace executive committees.

Accountability Will Improve

Accountability will be a major factor in organizational reviews and restructurings. The aim will be to strengthen the chain of accountability that runs from the staff to the members by way of the officers and board. Weaknesses in the chain, such as relationships between staff and committee chairs that undercut accountability, will be rectified. There will be a more annual reporting to the members on the status of operations and programs, similar to reporting procedures of publicly held corporations. These moves will strengthen the role of the staff and help to shift the leadership mode toward the staff-driven end of the spectrum.

New Consensus Mechanisms Will Develop

In order to avoid polarizations that immobilize an organization, associations will increasingly develop mechanisms, processes, and intra-organizational relationships for achieving consensus and for handling disagreements. There will be emphasis on solving problems by incorporating positions of both sides to avoid win-lose situations. There will be less emphasis on developing rigid positions and more emphasis on clarifying the interests of the association and its members, particularly as associations form coalitions.[18]

Trade and Professional Associations Will Serve as Models

As the profession of association management grows, the CSEs of philanthropic associations will look to the world of large trade and professional associations for information, training, and professional relationships. Present separation will give way to integration. Associations that offer education in association management will be seen as major sources of training and support.

Areas for Further Study

This study has examined one aspect of the leadership of associations, the relationships between staff and volunteers. The analysis, in highlighting distinguishing characteristics of associations that are staff-driven, volunteer-driven, or balanced in their leadership mode, also suggests additional areas for further study, enumerated next.

More needs to be known about philanthropic associations and how they function. Less is understood about these associations than about trade and professional associations. The similarities and differences among various kinds of philanthropic associations and their relationships to trade and professional associations deserve extensive study.

How can associations exercise leadership in industry and the professions? How have associations developed the agreements and courses of action needed to enable their members to function more responsibly and with a longer time horizon? What associations have successfully alerted members to the dangers and risks of their own behavior, and how have they effected changes?

How do associations successfully resolve differences that have the potential for polarizing the members? What processes have associations developed that result in win-win solutions to controversial public policy questions?

More work needs to be done on the life cycles of associations, not in the context of their leadership modes, but concerning their organizational structures, ability to get work done, relationships with members, and ability to wield influence.

What are the criteria for success of chief elected officers in staff- and volunteer-driven associations? What are their backgrounds and characteristics? Are there ways that associations can choose volunteer leaders appropriate to the times?

The decision-making processes in associations need to be better understood. For example, lacking such business criteria as return on investment, what forms the bases for decisions about the allocation of resources? How does a significant change in the proportion of nondues income to total revenue affect the decision-making process?

The whole question of productivity in associations needs to be examined. How should productivity be measured? How can it be improved? What is the effect of leadership modes on productivity? What opportunities help staff to function like a team?

Investigation of these types of questions will expand the knowledge about associations and make them an even more powerful and positive force in our society.

Notes

1. Two excellent sources of information about the types of associations are Tracy D. Conners, ed., *The Nonprofit Organization Handbook* (New York: McGraw-Hill Book Co., 1980), 1-3—1-15 and Theodore Levitt, *The Third Sector: New Tactics for a Responsive Society* (New York: AMACOM, 1973), 48-69.

2. John Kenneth Galbraith, *The Anatomy of Power* (Boston: Houghton Mifflin Co., 1983), 24-37.

3. Alexis de Tocqueville, *Democracy in America*, vol. 2 (New York: Random House, 1945), 115.

4. Galbraith, *Anatomy of Power*, 24-37.

5. Philip Kotler, *Marketing for Nonprofit Organizations* (Englewood Cliffs, NJ: Prentice-Hall, 1982), 488-515.

6. *National Trade and Professional Associations of the United States*, 15th ed. (New York: Columbia Books, 1980).

7. Peter F. Drucker, *Management* (New York: Harper & Row, 1973), 61.

8. American Society of Association Executives, *Association Operating Ratio Report, 1988-89* (Washington, D.C., ASAE, 1989).

9. Robert Campbell, *Fisherman's Guide: A Systems Approach to Creativity and Organization* (Boston: New Science Library, 1985), 313-22.

10. de Tocqueville, *Democracy in America*, 117. [The same volume number as in the preceding note.]

11. Robert Anthony and Regina Herzlinger, *Management and Control in Nonprofit Organizations* (Homewood, IL: Richard D. Irwin, 1975), chapters 1–4.

12. Charles N. Waldo, *Boards of Directors* (Westport, CT: Quorum Books, 1985), 16–35.

13. Edgar H. Schein, *Organizational and Cultural Leadership* (San Francisco: Jossey-Bass Publishers, 1986), 331–27.

14. Foundation of the American Society of Association Executives, ''Critical Competencies of Association Executives,'' (Foundation of the American Society of Association Executives, Washington, D.C., 1988, photocopy), 30.

15. Ibid.

16. Ibid., 31.

17. Ibid. [The same page as in the preceding note.]

18. Roger Fisher and William Ury, *Getting to Yes* (Boston: Houghton Mifflin Co., 1981).

Other Publications Available from The ASAE Foundation

The Personal Equation: A Critical Look at Executive Competency in Associations

Researchers interviewed over 100 top association executives to discover the critical characteristics of success. These characteristics are presented in order of rank importance in several major category areas such as fiscal management, long-range planning, etc. The workbook format is supplemented with an overview report of the study results. Catalog No. 213501.

Association International Activity

Sixteen case studies explore the success (and failures) of associations that have become international organizations. Specific examples of planning international meetings, dealing with cultural differences, and developing a global membership are included. Catalog No. 216276.

The Liability Crisis and the Use of Volunteers by Non-Profit Associations

This study, conducted by The Gallup Organization, explores how associations have dealt with the liability crisis, how it has changed their programs and affected participation. Catalog No. 213700.

Future Perspectives

Fourteen highly respected association chief staff executives share their views on topics as diverse as entrepreneurism, the new breed of volunteer leader, and management in transition. Catalog No. 216177.

Future Forces

Explore the successful strategies that will turn tomorrow's explosive growth and change to your best advantage. This bestseller examines how the future is taking shape now. Catalog No. 216175.

To order one of these publications call ASAE Publications (202) 626–2748.